FULL FACE TO (

FULL FACE TO GOD

An Introduction to the Enneagram

David Mahon

Illustrations by Bernard Atherton

Matthew James Publishing

First published in 1998 by
Darton, Longman and Todd Ltd

This revised edition published in 2003 by
Matthew James Publishing Ltd
19 Wellington Close
Chelmsford, Essex CM1 2EE
www.matthew-james.co.uk

ISBN 1–898366 77 2

A catalogue record for this book is available
from the British Library.

Cover design by Peter Robb
Phototypeset in 9.5/12.5pt Palatino by Intype London Ltd
Printed and bound in Great Britain by
J W Arrowsmith, Bristol, Avon

Contents

There is nobody who escapes the system.

1

INTRODUCTION
Encounter with the Enneagram

Within every heart abide angels and devils.

Leonardo Boff

The Enneagram is a route to self-appreciation. As we work with it, play and laugh with it, we come to know ourselves as different, gifted and powerful. The price we pay for this knowing is inner endeavour.

The Enneagram way is a profoundly spiritual tool. It was originally nurtured as a broadsword of spiritual direction and this remains its greatest strength.

This is a basic Enneagram book. It is intended for pupils of the inner way who have no knowledge, or only scant awareness, of the Enneagram's richness. It makes no attempt to theorise, advance or recast the system. Others are doing this to good effect. Here, the intention is to integrate and present in gentle format the best of the Enneagram's wisdom tradition, combining psychological and spiritual insights in a Christian context.

The origins of the Enneagram personality system are steeped in mystery. Some of its advocates have claimed it to be at least 2000 years old, but until the 1960s this wisdom was handed down only by word of mouth. Now at last it is being opened up, developed and shared.

As a route to personal growth and healing, the Enneagram offers us a practical means of discovering the strengths and weaknesses of our personality and offers us precise pointers for further growth. It helps us to understand our problems and our relationships with family and friends.

The Enneagram (the word is Greek and means 'nine aspects')

teaches us to receive reality objectively. It is a bold listing of the ways we play out our lives and how we attempt to persuade other people – and even God – to approve our viewpoint. It probes personal and communal depths and ultimately can make us capable of reaching out to something other than ourselves.

The truth of the Enneagram way is always in the tasting. While awakening us to self-truth, it cannot undertake for us the work which this demands. Real self-knowledge calls for some effort. We will be offered here an insight into our own performance and our place in the world, and, as the presentation of this book highlights, we will be called on at key moments to smile at ourselves – even to laugh heartily. The smiles and the laughter, and maybe the tears, will, in part at least, be our ways of coping with the joy of the discoveries we make and the inevitable humiliations we will experience along this path.

After a hidden gestation period, the Enneagram system is being seen as a gift to our times. But the process offers more than a quick-fix personality profile. It is capable of revealing to us the story that underpins our life. That is why it can be so humiliating and energising. It points us in the direction of a more authentic relationship with ourselves, with others and with God. It shows us how we can enhance our psychological and spiritual search. All of us are invited to set out on this journey of self-knowledge. We have a whole lifetime to do it. At the ordinary level we need to know what makes us tick. What is really motivating us, or blocking us, at the core of our being? Why do we do what we do? What are our personal strengths and weaknesses? These are the territories of the Enneagram.

The process nurtures self-observation. It invites us to ongoing discernment. We stand back and watch ourselves. We can observe the workings of our mind, the rise and fall of our moods and our passions. Rich in paradox and yet lucid in its application, the Enneagram opens us up to our personal and limited bias, our compulsive way of looking at life.

The Judeo-Christian tradition cherishes the human person as made in the image and likeness of God. Each of us is unique. As individuals we have our special gifts and talents, our endearing qualities and powerful attributes. These gifts to personality are blessings to rejoice in, virtues to live out, strengths to exercise. They are given to each individual, and through each person, they become resources at the service of the community. The Enneagram recognises that each of the nine human personality types has within them a positive reservoir of these gifts.

Unfortunately, it turns out that our gift – that which is special to us – also has destructive potential. Owing to the strength of our gifts, we begin to identify early and intensely with what we are good at and, often, we find ourselves fixated on the resulting self-image.

Awareness brings to light not only our giftedness, but also the patterns of our personality dipped in addictions and conditioning. These are part of our nature. Initially, we don't even recognise some of these as a problem. This shadow side of our personality includes our compulsions, our masks, our dysfunctional patterns of behaviour, and what turns out to be a hidden and central blindness. This is the undetected shadow that stands poised to blanket our personality and poison our authenticity. Fortunately, the Enneagram allows us to see the hidden sources of our brokenness.

We begin to understand how we carefully construct defences to keep this shadow side of ourselves at bay. These hidden forces can be so entrenched that we are not consciously aware of them. They amount to a core set of responses, starkly resistant to change, against which we can become quite powerless.

Initially we co-opt this darkness as a strategic and limiting process of self-protection. It can become a strategy for self-salvation. It keeps our truest self at a distance. It is the dark side of our gift. The Enneagram teaches us that we are all capable of over-identifying with our virtues to the point of utter destruction. We all have a natural focus which we promote and develop. This becomes our compulsive worldview. Most of us have great difficulty recognising the truth of our compulsion. It feeds our self-image and, at the same time, it short-changes the world and defines it as deficient. This is sin in the classic sense. Our gift becomes our darkness. We may avoid this truth, and when we do so, we allow other people to create our agenda. We have to learn to sharpen our awareness and craft our dispassion in order to prevent our gift from engulfing us.

How do we deal with our darkness? Our key is to befriend.

There is no call here for subjugation. Our blindness is not an enemy to be vanquished, but an essential void within that calls out for urgent accommodation. Our real gift is our sin acknowledged, tamed and redeemed by grace. We have to embrace our gift in order to see our sin. We have to unmask our false self in order to experience the real dimension of our giftedness. It amounts to a healing transformation.

Understanding becomes a catalyst for self-acceptance. Once the instinct which we have exaggerated into compulsion assumes proper proportion in our lives, it invites us to a new freedom, a new 'at homeness' with our giftedness and our compulsions.

The compelling wisdom of the Enneagram system forces us to be honest with ourselves. Along the way of transformation it creates an inner observer which is truthful and compassionate. It reveals our essential selves and encourages us to accept and work with what we see. These are crucial steps in our journey into self-appreciation. The psychological and the spiritual in us travel hand in hand. The system confirms that we are whole, holistic and holy.

There is nobody who escapes the system. All of us have our dysfunctional patterns. Nobody is quite sure how we acquire our specific bias, but by the time we are four years of age most of us have chosen our addiction. And it stays with us. A good deal of the rest of our journey is spent coming to terms with it.

Many of us never really acknowledge our compulsion or begin to deal with it. Many suffer needlessly as a result of this neglect and significant potential is thwarted.

The Enneagram remains a compendium of inclusiveness. There are huge democratic factors at play in the system. Our compulsion succeeds both in gifting us and blinding us. It offers us a virtue and at the same time it dumps us with a shadow. There are nine of these compulsions and this book will help you to discover which one is yours.

Some Enneagram adherents contend it was an original Sufi (charismatic Muslim) insight that there were nine constant aspects of personality that could act as a gift or as a restriction on people as they opened up their search psychologically and spiritually. The Sufis called their model of guidance the Face of God. They saw each of these nine possible personalities as a refraction of the one divine source.

Enneagram wisdom can therefore be readily matched with traditional religious routes of spiritual guidance. It can help us to be real about ourselves; the blessed and the broken within us. This is an enterprise that all of us can undertake.

The Enneagram will highlight our gift – what it is about us that makes us who we are. This is intended to serve as a highly supportive insight. We may have travelled a considerable way without this recognition. But before this breakthrough happens some detective work, some discernment, some honesty will be called for. One of the aims of this book is to help readers to recognise with precision the space they occupy on the Enneagram wheel. I will present in some detail the positive and negative aspects of the nine personality types highlighted in the system. These nine types can be described as follows:

One: The Perfectionist
Two: The Giver
Three: The Achiever
Four: The Artist
Five: The Observer
Six: The Supporter
Seven: The Optimist
Eight: The Leader
Nine: The Mediator

When you have detected your own personality type – and there is no need to rush the process – this insight will be developed with the aim of making it an abiding reference point of strength and growth for you.

This process of self-discovery can be highly effective in the challenge it offers and the changes it helps to bring about. There are two prerequisites – patience and a sense of humour. Armed with this particular duo all of us can continue to travel with good purpose along the Enneagram route.

I have every confidence that the delightful drawings of my colleague Bernard Atherton, who has enlivened this book with his mischievous cartoons, will add to the enjoyment you experience on this journey.

Nothing short of transformation is the goal.

2

DETECTING YOUR PERSONALITY TYPE

People are born equal but they are also born different.
Erich Fromm

The Enneagram challenges us to confront what is hidden, the compulsions that drive us, and then invites us to step beyond these entanglements into a new freedom. As we shall see, nothing short of transformation is the goal.

One of the most beautiful aspects of the Enneagram, beyond its basic description of the nine different character types and the naming of our gift, is the support it offers us when we face up to the negative aspects of our personality. It is a powerful tool for confronting our shadow.

The Enneagram names us as partial, broken people and provokes our acceptance of this reality. With this realisation and submission, a simplicity and sense of truth unfolds for each of us. We learn to stop defending our excess of self. This is why the Enneagram is a spiritual conversion path. It underlines the Christian dictum that we have to die to ourselves in order to live to ourselves. In the same way, our enemies turn out to be our best friends.

Our shadow is the other side of our gift. Both the gift and the shadow contribute to our energy. The Enneagram will define and highlight our bogus energy for us. But best of all, the system points each of us in the direction of a new capacity, a new freedom. It possesses an inner energy that guides us to our individual path of change and conversion. We often discover that a persistent aspect of our personality has been blocking untapped strength. In this sense the gift and the shadow sit together and they need to be unscrambled.

The Enneagram is one of several personality profile methods that direct us towards self-knowledge. Like the Myers-Briggs Type Indicator it is not a specifically Christian instrument, but both these systems are helpful tools for Christians and non-Christians to use. You need no prior knowledge to benefit from the Enneagram's creative way.

In their quest for transformation, Christians will ask: How can we break ourselves open to the healing power of Christ? Teresa of Avila, that Spanish saint of tempestuous energy, had this to say about self-knowledge: 'Knowing ourselves is something so important that I wouldn't want any relaxation ever in this regard however high you may have climbed. . . . Never, however exalted the soul may be, is anything else more fitting than self-knowledge . . . without it everything goes wrong.' Summing up her teaching on self-knowledge in her classic work *The Interior Castle,* Teresa bluntly declared: 'All our trials and disturbances come from not understanding ourselves.'

Many people initially have difficulty matching their own personality with one of the types outlined in the Enneagram system. Most of us at first are convinced there is a slice of ourselves in several of the types. There is some truth in this viewpoint, but don't let it put you off. There is one face – which often stubbornly resists recognition – that matches your own personality with precision. For that reason, and to assist your search further, as well as beginning to offer a means of comparison, listed below are the root stances of the Enneagram types. Initially, you may not understand all the headings given below each type, but the listing will eventually prove helpful and will assist reference.

At first sight, you may not be able to spot your own personality, or you may more readily glimpse similarities between the types and some of your family members, friends or co-workers. This is a gentle and practical way of letting yourself into the system. If you start to recognise that the personality trends described are real – and match them to people you know – you can begin to acknowledge the truth which the system reflects and its harmony, and this makes for a good beginning.

The truth factor is vital. If there is no integrity or consistency in the descriptions of personality, it would be unlikely that any genuine or lasting benefits would be experienced when we come to use the system as a route of acceptance, change and conversion – and that's what the Enneagram is really about.

Here are some basic descriptions of the nine Enneagram personalities:

FACE ONE: The Perfectionist
My way: Seeking perfection
My statement: 'I work hard.'
My centre: Gut
My passion: Anger
My compulsion: Perfection
My fear: What's less than the best
My avoidance: Open anger
My method: Criticism
My need: To let go, to relax
My virtue: Serenity

The Enneagram is a powerful tool for confronting our shadow.

FACE TWO: The Giver
My way: Seeking to help
My statement: 'I care.'
My centre: Heart
My passion: Pride
My compulsion: Helping others
My fear: Having no role
My avoidance: What I need
My method: Empathy
My need: To discover self-worth
My virtue: Humility

FACE THREE: The Achiever
My way: Seeking to achieve
My statement: 'I am successful.'
My centre: Heart
My passion: Deceit
My compulsion: Efficiency
My fear: Failure
My avoidance: Failure
My method: Image
My need: To see through the image
My virtue: Truth

FACE FOUR: The Artist
My way: Seeking to create
My statement: 'I am unique.'
My centre: Heart
My passion: Envy
My compulsion: To be different
My fear: The ordinary
My avoidance: The mundane
My method: Creative expression
My need: Sense of reality
My virtue: Equanimity

FACE FIVE: The Observer
My way: Observing
My statement: 'I am perceptive.'
My centre: Head
My passion: Greed
My compulsion: Knowledge
My fear: Meaninglessness
My avoidance: Emptiness
My method: Observation
My need: To be involved
My virtue: Detachment

FACE SIX: The Supporter
My way: Supporting
My statement: 'I am loyal.'
My centre: Head
My passion: Doubt and anxiety
My compulsion: Security
My fear: Fear
My avoidance: Originality
My method: Authority and danger
My need: Faith
My virtue: Courage

FACE SEVEN: The Optimist
My way: Optimism
My statement: 'I am cheerful.'
My centre: Head
My passion: Gluttony
My compulsion: Idealism
My fear: Pain
My avoidance: Pain
My method: Planning for good times
My need: Balance
My virtue: Temperance

FACE EIGHT: The Leader
My way: Leadership
My statement: 'I am strong.'
My centre: Gut
My passion: Lust
My compulsion: To be in charge
My fear: Weakness
My avoidance: Subordination
My method: Power
My need: Tenderness
My virtue: Simplicity

FACE NINE: The Mediator
My way: Mediation
My statement: 'I am content.'
My centre: Gut
My passion: Laziness
My compulsion: Inactivity
My fear: Conflict
My avoidance: Conflict
My method: Peace
My need: Action
My virtue: Diligence

Gut types are apt to view life as a battleground.

3

THREE BASIC CENTRES OF ENERGY

What seems different in yourself; that's the rare thing you possess. The one thing that gives each of us worth and that's just what we try to suppress. And we claim to love life.

André Gide

One of the most fascinating divisions in the Enneagram system is the Head-Heart-Gut triad. These energies offer direct clues to your own dynamic as you gather evidence about which of the nine types mirrors your own personality.

All of us are familiar with – and occupy – these three 'centres of being' – the head, the heart and the gut. We all dip into these three spaces quite frequently. Our thinking and planning takes us into the head, our values system takes us into the heart and when we use intuition, we are said to be 'coming from the gut'. But the fact is that all of us occupy one of these centres to the detriment of the other two. This basic divison may therefore help us to place ourselves, or at least limit our choice, to three places on the system.

We can, for example, describe FIVE, SIX and SEVEN types on the Enneagram as head people. Their control centre – the one they occupy most of the time – is the head. They are strong on thinking, as opposed to feeling (heart) or intuition (gut). In any new situation, the inclination of the head person is to step back, take in the evidence and use logic. They tackle assignments methodically and may attempt to construct patterns of meaning. They are inclined to overlook their feelings and can remain objectively uninvolved.

Types TWO, THREE and FOUR are the heart people – the social animals. Whereas people in the head space are inclined to move away from people, heart types naturally move towards other people. They are concerned to be with others. They function on the level of feelings. Touch and taste are important to them. They regard relationships as a task to be confronted and mastered. In a new situation they are likely to ask: 'Do you like me?'

To live at this feeling level is experienced by heart types as the way of achieving personal encounter with others. Prestige and image are usually important to heart people, but they can be ruled by what others think about them. They can also repress their aggressions and hide behind a facade of kindness and action. They may appear as self-confident and stylish, but inwardly they can also feel incapable and ashamed. In the religious sphere they tend towards forms of worship that are bound up with groups or social interaction.

The gut people occupy EIGHT, NINE and ONE stances on the Enneagram. Gut people, as you would expect, act instinctively. They don't have to process through their head or their heart. They function with instinct and habits. In a new situation they are inclined to say: 'Here I am; deal with me.'

These gut types are apt to view life as a battleground. They move spontaneously, often in reaction to an external stimulus. They can be concerned, even unconsciously, with issues of power and justice. They can also be ruled by aggression and often insist on standing their own ground. When things go badly for them, they tend to shoulder the blame. Anxiety and fear are hidden behind a cover of self-assertion. They can easily strike a pose of strength, but may be inwardly tormented by self-doubt.

If you are attempting to discover or clarify your own place on the Enneagram, it may be useful to try to place yourself initially according to this head-heart-gut division. Success here restricts your choice to three stances.

Patience and some sifting of evidence is required.

4

THE DILEMMA WITHIN

Attempts to hide your streakiness will sometimes be successful, always dishonest.

Anthony de Mello

Self-knowledge will always be a precious commodity. Most of us know from our own experience that without fundamental insight our development is likely to remain a hit-and-miss affair. To start out on this journey of knowing self, we need a genuine perception into our real strengths and weaknesses. We need to know, for example, what motivates us, and what it is that curbs and prevents our involvement. Only when we know why we do what we do, are we really beginning to direct and control our undertakings.

The Enneagram system will also readily demonstrate how easy it is for us to hoodwink ourselves. One of the faces of the Enneagram matches our own personality with precision and each of the nine energies are presented here in some detail to help us to discern the energies, both positive and negative, belonging to each personality type. As we begin to grapple with these energies, we need to remember that we are not dealing merely with stereotypes. The system is always far more than a static measure of personality. For each type it represents a route to healing and personal growth.

While highlighting for us some of the inner work we will need to undertake, the Enneagram will never do this work for us. Growth comes when we face up to the specific dilemma which exists for each personality type within the system. Possessing the advantage of having been developed over time and within a spiritual tradition, the Enneagram system also turns out to be incisive, practical and good fun.

So far we have provided only basic descriptions of the personality types. These will now be presented with additional detail and pointers given to the inner dynamic that begins to mark out the personal path of change and conversion. These routes challenge us to hunt out and eventually come to terms with the compulsion that drives each one of us. Equally they urge us to open up to our own rich potential. Remember, there is nobody who escapes the system, and nothing short of transformation is the goal. The shadow or 'sin' side of our personality is surprisingly hinged to our gift. There is a paradox or dilemma within each personality and we will be taking a close look at each one of these.

Making the match

I have followed the traditional way of describing the nine personality types in the Enneagram system by using numbers. None of us, of course, is a number.

The Enneagram route is an attempt to find truth, and the truth, as we well know, when realised, can be difficult to take. You may well awaken to your own reluctance. The descriptions of the nine personalities are representative. They don't encapsulate a total picture of any particular individual. We are all unique and the Enneagram respects this miracle. Nevertheless, the system highlights individual and group tendencies with remarkable accuracy. These traits, which we hold in common with others in our personality grouping, have been drawn vividly to help the reader grasp the specific energies at work.

You may feel you can see aspects of yourself in several types described by the Enneagram, and this, as I have suggested, contains much truth. But in the end you will come to detect that one type – both the positive and negative aspects of that type – describes your personality with precision. Initially, it is often not easy to recognise this, or to acknowledge it when you do, so patience and some sifting of the evidence is therefore required. It is important not to rush this process, but to relax, perhaps, and enjoy the chase. Involve your friends; they may be able to help you.

The Perfectionist

5

FACE ONE

The Perfectionist

Reformer, Activist, Idealist, Teacher, Moralist, Visionary, Challenger, Organiser, Coach and Ascetic

It is a splendid habit to laugh inwardly at yourself. It is the best way of regaining your good humour and of finding God without further anxiety.

Abbé de Tourville

My way: Seeking perfection
My statement: 'I work hard.'
My centre: Gut
My passion: Anger
My compulsion: Perfection
My fear: What's less than the best
My avoidance: Open anger
My method: Criticism
My need: To let go, to relax
My virtue: Serenity

Gift

The gift of the ONE personality motivates them to improve things. They are independent, dutiful and responsible. Idealists and normally well-organised, they take great pride in a job well done. They have the ability to prioritise, set high standards and can dedicate themselves to worthwhile causes. They are keen to clarify and convey detailed information. They make excellent teachers and are compassionate to the disadvantaged.

As children ONEs may have come to the conclusion that they have to work hard. They strive to be very good. They seek to discover the rules and attempt to follow them. In this way they hope to win approval. The rules also give them a ready standard by which they can judge others. Criticism can have an impact on their self-image and they may become resentful and serious.

ONEs can be communicative and lively company. They are idealists and make good teachers, administrators and leaders. However, their constant search for perfection can make others feel uncomfortable. They are punctual, tidy, meticulous, methodical and hard-working. They can readily become workaholics.

They are prone to anger but may deny its existence, opting to seethe just below the surface. They attempt to keep a damper on their hostility. This repressed anger can boil over into resentment.

People of this personality type feel a need within themselves to be right, and they may also have a tendency to compel those around them to toe the line. They can be self-righteous and intolerant.

ONE personalities can be critical of themselves because nothing ever quite matches up to their hopes and expectations. They are prone to worry and often find themseves and those around them difficult to live with. They are sticklers for detail, strive to put everything in apple-pie order and inevitably never achieve the perfection they are looking for.

Their strongly critical inner voice can be relentless. They are often uptight and serious. They have to use considerable energy in keeping their emotions under control. They can appear sullen. They are constrained by time and can be frustrated when their high expectations of themselves, and of others, are not reached or maintained. They are constantly on the lookout for improvements. They may become compulsive about trying to reach these high standards.

ONEs can be impatient and stubborn when it comes to getting their own way. The tension they carry around makes it difficult for them to relax and let go.

ONEs will be inclined to say 'yes' to most of the following statements:

- I like to be right. I have high moral standards.
- If I waste time it makes me feel uneasy.
- I try to be on time; it sets the right tone.
- I can be quite restless and strive for the unobtainable.
- I am well organised and dependable.
- Most judgments are either right or wrong.
- I'm seldom completely satisfied with myself or the job in hand.
- I can let a minor flaw ruin the whole thing for me.
- I feel obliged to let people know when they get things wrong.
- I put considerable effort into correcting my faults.

Challenges confronting The Perfectionist

When we reflect on the central dilemmas facing the nine personalities in the Enneagram system, it is important not to lose sight

'I work hard.'

of the positive aspects of each of these types. We are dealing here with some of the negative aspects because these sit close to the dilemmas which have to be faced if change and transformation are to be embraced. The precise way of conversion will be considered later.

The Enneagram system is paradoxical. The negative must always be held in balance with the positive. To neglect or to accentuate either side is to obscure the total picture.

ONEs are often disappointed because people, events and life itself never quite match up to expectations. Most frustrating of all, ONEs are disappointed by their own imperfection. For this reason the route of religion can be attractive to them. When everybody disappoints, God at least is perfect.

ONEs are conscientious, dutiful and responsible. They used to be good little boys and girls. Now they are great believers in achieving excellence, irrespective of the costs involved. In the cause of a top performance they are prepared to punish themselves. They are driven by time and are exacting about punctuality. Their own internal critic is a hard task-master and they are inclined to give it undue attention.

ONEs are also prone to be serious and puritanical. Fun is only possible when all the duties have been well executed – and the duties are endless. Even free time is inclined to unfold as one more opportunity for yet another bout of self-improvement.

They are resentful if those close to them, at home or at work, don't meet the highest standards. Their irritation can be intense. The imperfection all around them makes them angry. Anger is the capital blindness of the ONE. But anger is a very imperfect trait. They therefore find it difficult to acknowledge the anger which motivates and drives them. They are also reluctant to admit, either to themselves or to others, any underlying resentment. A saturating resentment can be at the heart of the dilemma faced by the ONE personality. Inside they may burn with rage because the world is so imperfect. But to acknowledge this anger is to join the imperfection. They can be wounded by even the suspicion that they are angry. They are in fact ashamed of their anger and therefore tend to bury it. But just below the surface it continues to simmer.

This perfection-prone personality can be caught up in the belief that there is only one right way to handle an assignment. They are also apt to believe they have a monopoly on the one right way. This lack of flexibility can make them stubborn and dictatorial. This is likely to boil over into an aggressive stance and the fact that they are unwilling to concede this will often add to the internal pressure. They live close to the edge of self-righteousness. Others sense this and often find it difficult to cope with. ONEs trigger a fight-or-flight response.

These forces, usually hidden, readily move them into work-aholism. They busy themselves endlessly in a determined attempt to let off their excessive steam. Taken to extremes, these inclinations can lead the neurotic ONE personality to preach morality and goodness and at the same time live immorally. The repressed shadow bursts out.

ONEs, like all of us, have several fronts on which they can carve out their liberation. Their enduring task is to free themselves from being over-critical. The precise dart which wounds the ONE personality is their own self-criticism.

They must learn to accept themselves and others without passing endless judgements about each and every detail, person and eventuality. Opening themselves to humour and allowing gratitude to arise will play a part in this growth process.

They constantly give off a negative current of energy. Without building relationships of understanding, acceptance and trust, the criticisms they resort to become too much for the people around them. Others will back off because of this critical attitude which may be experienced as debilitating. The constant carping does not serve the cause of enlightenment or joy.

Perfectionism is essentially a denial of true love. ONEs have to discover that they are angry as they chase after what in fact they already possess – God's love and acceptance. In that knowledge they can at last drop their pseudo-morality stance.

Hooks of the ONE

- A torrent of self-criticism.
- A compulsive need to act on what seems to be correct; in excess, a do-gooder.

- Procrastination in decision-making, stemming from the fear of making a mistake.

Route of integration for The Perfectionist

See Appendix 1: The Conversion Enterprise.

ONEs have to unlearn their conviction, or compulsion, that there is only one possible mode of operation – their way. This is true for all of us, of course, but it is particularly true for the ONE personality. This painful route starts as they come to terms with their anger. The source of this anger points to their compulsion.

When ONEs begin to detect and then dismember their judgementalism, as well as their persistent dictatorial behaviour and resentments, it then becomes possible for them to move towards the gentler route of compassion.

If they can at least occasionally drop their need to be dutiful,

They attempt to keep a damper on their hostility.

and begin to see through themselves and their insistence on doing things in what they regard as the one right way, it becomes possible for them to ease up on themselves, to enjoy life a little and even to celebrate.

ONEs are friendly when they don't take themselves too seriously. Their greatest freedom – and it is the crucial road to freedom for all of us – is to be able to laugh at themselves. Only then will the need for absolutes and the self-righteousness be punctured. Only then will they begin to see that there is more than one way to skin all those proverbial cats. Laughter is their essential grace. When the ONE personality laughs heartily, they begin to see themselves in perspective, but they can experience great difficulty coming to this enlightenment.

Having reached this new perspective, however, the ONE begins to understand that his or her viewpoint is only part of the picture. Their monopoly on goodness, certitude and correctness finally slackens. The ONE personality eventually comes to sense that their hold on reality is limited and considerably more confined than they had previously imagined. By degrees, and from their own experience, they are required to come to terms with the fact that all aspects of life will always be imperfect. Integration, wholeness (holiness) has to be seen as a process of growth rather than as an attainment of the highest standards.

Along this route, ONEs can learn to live in greater serenity, more generously and in peace with those around them – letting God be God – instead of constantly imposing their own rigid view of perfection. When this transformation process begins, grace is at work and humility at play.

ONEs have to back off enough to observe the imperfection in the world around them. The gift of the spirit that marks the healthy person is always the opposite of the capital sin. In the ONE, therefore, the fruit is a positive tranquillity.

How do we move from repressed anger to harmony? It may be important to acknowledge personal aggression and, even more crucially, not to take our anger – and the causes of our anger – too seriously. God loves us the way we are. He loves us before we have made any effort. Genuine friendships, contact with nature and a graceful appreciation of the genuine blessings in our lives can also help to urge on this integration.

To bring about conversion ONEs need to embrace the best aspects of the SEVEN. This will help them to:

- relax and not take things too seriously. They need to be less rigid and stop overworking. They need to enjoy themselves.
- begin to acknowledge their anger and see the importance of not living it out.
- open up to their feelings – the messy and inappropriate ones which they seek to control. They have to come to terms with limitations – their own and other people's.
- stop judging themselves and others by the rule book. They need to be more patient and less rigid.
- recognise and appreciate the principles of growth. Mistakes are a normal part of the way people grow. This is a process which takes time and calls for patience.

The Perfectionist: Symbols and Invitation

Symbols are usually used in the Enneagram as a lighthearted description of the major energies reflected by the different personalities. But by drawing on the intuitive discernment of Sister Mary Helen Kelley, a member of the Poor Clare monastic community in Memphis, Tennessee, USA, a new depth of understanding and refinement has been brought to these symbols. I have attempted here to faithfully portray some of her insights relating to the animal and country categories for each type, starting with the Perfectionist.

Animal: Eagle

The eagle expresses its brilliance in high-soaring flight. It is a universal symbol of courage and power. The eagle tendency is to rest seldom. It cherishes its mountain perch, enjoys keenness of vision and has the unusual hawk capacity to see in colour. Proud and aggressive, the eagle, experiencing life as it does from a high perspective, is identified with the symbol of the good knight. The eagle person supports moral order, the law, country and God.

Country: Ireland and Israel
These countries share a sense of being chosen by God. In both of them a mood of righteousness wrestles with darkness and evil. In Ireland Catholics and Protestants have long struggled with each other, and Jews and Arabs have consistently fought with each other in Israel. Historically these countries have been unwilling to take their place peaceably with the rest of the world. Both countries, although small, harbour a spirit of difference and challenge to the world community. Both are missionary in their zeal.

Colour: Silver is the symbolic colour of the ONE. It is cool and clear-cut. ONEs mirror this clear, sharp presence. The integrated ONE stands for growth and renewal, by the light of the moon.

Beliefs

- Life (myself, my job, my relationships, just about everything) is never quite good enough.
- Good times must be earned and deserved.
- Suffering is inevitable.
- If things are easy, not much is really being achieved.

Queries

- Is my performance good enough?
- What's next?
- What's wrong with this?
- Have I done enough?

Childhood message: 'Be good and stay out of trouble.' ONEs may have experienced themselves as the focus of critical attention or punishment. They are likely to have been given some responsibilities but few rewards.

Invitation: Towards growth

With surrender – ultimately to God – the ONE begins to accept the idea of growth as a process and not just as a virtue that has to be immediately acquired and demonstrated. Instead of looking for what has gone wrong, they begin to detect some good in the situation, however small. In this way they encounter serenity and begin to see harmony at play in creation.

The perfect God, the God of compassion, is patient and allows time for this growth and change. The Franciscan Richard Rohr, who has written in detail about his own ONEness, suggests that as the ONE personality begins to allow for and attain this growth, they come to 'share in the divine tranquillity'. Even the familiar energy of the ONE – often experienced by others as a destructive anger – can be transformed into a 'righteous indignation'.

Among the goals of the ONE is the unlearning of the centrality of duty and moderation of the endless quest to improve the world. God is offering us unconditional love. Unlearning is always part of the invitation. For ONEs it allows them to bring in fun, enjoyment and even communal celebration. As they let their resentments subside, true compassion becomes available.

The ONE personality is called to wholeness, to be fully alive. This is a love that includes limitations and true appreciation of a potential that may have already been achieved.

Jesus as teacher and reformer

See Appendix 2: The Nine Enlightenments.

The aim here is to demonstrate how Jesus lived through all nine personality types of the Enneagram and remained free of any compulsive edge.

As we have seen, the temptation of the ONE personality is towards perfection. For ONEs, a crucial paradox, highlighted in the Christian story, is how we become perfect (are made whole and therefore holy) by accepting our own imperfection.

There is a danger for ONEs that they struggle on with that erroneous translation from the Sermon on the Mount: 'Be perfect, as your Father in heaven is perfect.' This translation has caused untold damage. 'Be perfect' needs to be translated 'be made holy'. Being perfect is the hook of the ONE. We can only begin to be integrated, made whole and holy, when we manage to accept our imperfection.

We recognise Jesus in the ONE personality as gifted teacher. This was a major thrust in his life's work. He was also practising what he preached: there was no double morality at play. Using story, parable and allegory to highlight his teachings, Jesus enabled his own life and example to form his disciples into a functional spiritual school.

We have already seen how anger is the major avoidance of the ONE personality. But in the gospel we see Jesus making no attempt to bottle up his anger or hide it behind a friendly facade. Neither did he condemn sinners and people on the margins. He refused to accept the condemnation of one person by another, but he also refused to tolerate damaging behaviour capable of luring people into ruin.

In this way the teaching of Jesus combines compassion and zeal. He merges unconditional acceptance with the challenge of a true reformer. Forgiveness and atonement are his keys to a repentance which liberates. When he saved the woman about to be stoned, Jesus said: 'I do not condemn you. Go now and do not sin again.'

The positive qualities of the ONE are mirrored in the idealism of Jesus. He saw a world needing enlightenment. Things were not as God wanted them to be. He took his stand against deception. But there is nothing moody or despondent in his energy and style, nothing compulsive.

His parables about growth are invitations to the ONE personality in particular to trust in the evolution of God's reign. There is always the danger that the stridency of the ONE will continue to curb and prevent patience, patience with oneself, with others – particularly those closest – and with God.

The gospel encounter with Jesus will help ONEs to guard against:

- resentment and repression of anger.
- being caught up in the imperfection all around them. Jesus urges them to allow the weeds and the wheat to grow together.
- obsession with detail. Jesus challenges the scribes and Pharisees who are exacting in the details, but miss the cosmic and more urgent calling.
- looking too critically; being harsh and judgemental. Jesus uses

strong words about judging others. His message accentuates forgiveness.

Jesus shows ONEs how to rejoice in:
- their innate love of truth, justice and fairness.
- a capacity to see things in perspective and then to inspire and lead others.
- an ability to detect the giftedness of others.
- the blessing of high energy and intensity.
- their natural defence of the downtrodden.

Spur: To change from angry improvers of the world into effective reformers and visionary teachers of truth and justice.

Way of prayer for The Perfectionist

See Appendix 3: Prayer and the Enneagram.

ONEs have an immediate aim in prayer. They want things to be right and therefore their response is direct. Relentless in the chase after justice, truth and moral order, they need to experience the peace of being calm in God's presence. This can come to them as a great blessing. They relax and let be.

In prayer they are aided by a comfortable posture. An icon or a symbol may be helpful to them to start this process. But the ONE personality has no need to pile up the words. Their favoured route is that of simplification.

It is good for the ONE just to come to the presence of God, to sit, to let be. They present themselves as they are, encountering God in the moment. Their natural prayer stance is a simple, quiet, peaceful being in God's presence. This prayer avoids ideas or concepts. It needs no intermediary. This is the prayer of gentle encounter.

A set time for prayer is helpful to the ONE. They are high-energy people and they may need to give attention to this slowing-down process, looking forward to their time of prayer. To aid concentration they need only the simplest of mantras.

ONEs have no requirement for feelings before God. No words, no images. Their way is the route of simplicity, of the will alone. This is the prayer of stillness, the prayer of the heart. They move towards receptivity and surrender. They can come to know God in the darkness and in the silence. Their longing for the truth will help them persevere. In the ground of their being they are attentive. This is effortless prayer.

This route will deliver them from their driven search for unrealistic perfection. They have to let their harsh attitudes to themselves and others melt away in the face of God's compassion. Judgementalism and moralising will lose their hold. ONEs are all the time learning to wait.

The ONE route to well-being

Unhealthy characteristics: inflexible, self-righteous, vengeful
Average characteristics: perfectionist, scrupulous, austere, judgemental
Redeemed characteristics: aware, composed, ethically outstanding, well-balanced, realistic
Values: equilibrium, fair play, justice, peace, freedom
Time tendency: past
Strongest senses: hearing, smell
Emotion least controlled: fear
Domination: power and control
Masks: resentment, jealousy
Problems: indecision, repression

The ONE surrenders

- I no longer demand impossible standards, either from myself or from others.
- I let go of my angry feelings. I release my impatience.
- I abandon my focus on what is wrong with things.

The ONE affirmations

- I affirm that I can now allow myself to enjoy life.
- I say 'yes' to the many things that other people can teach me.

They need to let go.

- I treat other people with respect and tenderness.

Pilgrim path for the ONE personality

The Perfectionist's route of longing

Each of the Enneagram routes has the potential to lead us to the heart of the Christian message – a Christlike, universal encounter through love and awareness.

The quest of the ONE personality in the Enneagram system is the route of longing. The perfectionist searches for the way of excellence, the route beyond comparison. They desire a world where everything is as it should be. As we have seen, this energy is relentless. It leads to an abiding dissatisfaction with things as they are. ONEs are mesmerised by the way things ought to be.

This desire is costly. It is a blindness but it is also a pointer to true virtue.

Ultimately, what we long for is what we become. ONEs must learn to refine and trust their longing and allow it to expand. This will take them into the world of universal values – of goodness, truth, justice and beauty. It will also plunge them into action.

The desire of the ONE is at root energising and preparatory for the highest involvement. But the longing is usually too small. It needs to move through and beyond the egocentric, past the demand for the gleaming doorstep, the tidy shelf, the tip-top presentation or whatever other punctilious performance is on the agenda.

The gift of the ONE comes close to precision and clarity and in the end this gift can be directed towards the highest ends. Eventually the longing of the ONE has to be free for the universal; in Christian terms this means the values of the Kingdom. This is why the path of longing is rooted in conversion and courage. It opens to the God of unconditional love.

God image

As ONEs move along their path of integration, their God image expands. God is no longer confined to the role of judge and evaluator, constantly ticking or crossing, marking all of us up or down in the great book.

When you meet a ONE

- Be straight: ONEs don't like being manipulated and they quickly recognise it if you try it.
- Ask open questions that could help them to locate their feelings.
- Remember, it is the logical content that attracts the ONE. Be cautious about overplaying the feeling content when presenting your own case. At the same time it is good to give space to the ONE to allow them to contact their feelings.
- Acknowledge your own mistakes. They find this reassuring.

- Engage them in banter, particularly when they take the initiative. This will lighten the situation all round.
- Don't take their dangerous-sounding threats personally. The anger often stems from another and quite hidden agenda.

The Giver

6

FACE TWO

The Giver

Helper, Friend-in-Need, Healer, Confidant, Pleaser, Guardian Angel, Lover, Co-worker, Auxiliary and Altruist

The heart benevolent and kind, the most resembles God.

Robert Burns

My way: Seeking to help
My statement: 'I care.'
My centre: Heart
My passion: Pride
My compulsion: Helping others
My fear: Having no role
My avoidance: What I need
My method: Empathy
My need: To discover self-worth
My virtue: Humility

Gift

The gift of the TWO personality motivates them to be cheerful, friendly and helpful. They enjoy giving of their time and energy and they can make people feel good about themselves. They like to adopt supportive roles and are dependable, generous and caring. People and relationships are important to them and at their best they are gentle, dependable and loving people.

As children the likelihood is that TWOs gravitated towards helping around the house. They share generously. They can see immediately what needs to be done and they volunteer. When they are rewarded or praised for tackling these jobs, they feel satisfied and remain on the lookout for more tasks to be accomplished.

They come to know the requirements of other people and begin to meet these needs. But they need to be needed. Their reward is approval and attention. People therefore recognise how conscientious they are and are willing to oblige them with endless duties and tasks to be fulfilled. TWOs automatically start to put others before themselves. They set out to please with a vengeance – and they succeed.

TWOs sense the requirements and feelings of others and they can respond and empathise. They can readily express emotion. They are caring and productive people who enjoy reaching out and touching others. But the empathy and the feelings usually relate only to others and not to themselves. While generous in many ways to others, and prepared to make sacrifices for others, they tend to neglect their own feelings and deny their own personal needs.

Their whole identity may begin to hang on the help and assistance they can offer to others. If other people, and these can be the people closest to them, do not provide them with needs to meet, they can begin to feel quite purposeless and abandoned. They can be deeply hurt when friends, relatives and neighbours fail to appreciate them.

TWOs may be seeking attention for themselves when they go out to meet the real or imagined needs of others. They can become skilled and manipulative at doing this. Failing to recognise their own needs, they seldom ask directly for favours. Because they can see the needs of those around them, they expect other people to be able to see their needs. They take rejection badly, and experience themselves as victims or even martyrs to the cause.

Although warm and attentive, they often find intimacy difficult. Much of their charm is meant for admiration and approval rather than deep friendship. TWOs have a longing to be loved and can therefore be subject to infatuation. If their compulsion takes control, they tend towards exhibitionism and being overdramatic.

They are so involved in meeting the requirements of others, that as these duties and commitments pile up, there is a real danger they will lose contact with their own personal needs. The provider can finish up drained, with little or nothing to give.

TWOs will be inclined to say 'yes' to most of the following statements:

- I like to rescue people when I see they're in trouble or in difficult situations.
- People often come to me for comfort and advice.
- The most important consideration is always love.
- Sometimes I feel victimised by others, as though I'm just being used by them.
- The people in my life are vital to me. It is hard for me to let them go.
- I'm almost compelled to help other people whether I like it or not.
- I sometimes help others and then resent myself for it.
- I would much prefer to give than to receive.

'I care.'

- I enjoy paying people compliments.
- I love others so that they in turn can love me.

Challenges confronting The Giver

Because TWOs so readily sense the needs of others, it is easier for them to relate to their personal needs when they are alone. It is an ongoing challenge for them to create this unattached solitude. In this separate state they can learn to think.

TWOs have to relax enough to know that they don't need to keep meeting other people's requirements. They are ensnared by their conviction that there is no way they can receive without giving. They circle endlessly for love. They flatter and they need to be flattered. TWOs experience delight in being needed. They put considerable effort into gaining approval. They want to feel important in other people's lives. They can come to believe their very survival depends on it.

The negative aspect of this is that they can manipulate others and make them dependent, precisely through their excessive concern. Their giving, therefore, includes a hidden self-interest and they are challenged to come alive to this.

They want people to depend on them, but they try for all their worth to be independent of others. They readily recognise and even go in search of the needs of others, but they can fail completely to acknowledge their own. They feel ashamed when they show their neediness. Pride fuels this reluctance.

The capital blindness of the TWO is pride. They hide the fact that they have basic personal needs. They have to detect that their giving is part of their obtaining. This requires humility which, if achieved, opens the way to the exercise of their real virtue – unconditional giving.

They desperately need permission to look their own personal needs in the eye. They suppress these needs and even project them on to others. They fear what might happen if their immense need for love and warmth were revealed. They want to be loved but they can have a hard time finding their own true centre.

In relationships too they set out to please others. They know how to present themselves in order to be accepted and liked, but because of their ability to switch selves at will, they can become uncertain as to which self in the end is real. This can produce deep feelings of uncertainty. They will ask: Who is the real me? TWOs will surrender themselves only when they are convinced the other person will accept them. They may initially aim to flatter and then develop the feeling they have been controlled.

Many TWOs experience difficulty in saying 'no'. Because of their excessive giving, they can also be under a compulsion to be used. On the other hand, if approval is withheld, or their efforts go unrecognised, TWOs can feel deflated. They are inclined to expect gratitude from everyone – even from God.

Because they are capable of postponing their own needs in the interests of pleasing others, they can readily become indispensable. Liaison with power and powerful people guarantees personal survival. They can also set out to ally themselves with people who are unobtainable. TWOs can readily pair with someone who is themselves dependent. In some cultures, women are conditioned to be TWOs.

The challenge facing the TWO is to allow themselves to be loved for who they are. They have to learn not to depend on the esteem of others. They must stop earning love in order to experience unconditional love. They have to come to experience at first hand that it is God who is the prime mover.

Hooks of the TWO

- Pride in coming to the rescue of others but refusing to acknowledge personal needs.
- Avoiding rejection and gaining approval.
- Feeling controlled by other people's needs.

Route of integration for The Giver

See Appendix 1: The Conversion Enterprise.

Just as the root sin of the TWO is pride, the redemption factor is humility. This brings the TWO to the recognition that their endless giving cannot be disconnected from their own needs. When they realise and accept that their giving is the other side of their possession – that the giving has real strings attached – the awakening can lead to dynamic change.

TWOs in the unredeemed state believe they are the most generous, lovable people in the world. But the reality includes the strings. When these are acknowledged, real transformation and freedom – and therefore real compassion – can begin to happen. TWOs must learn to say an emphatic 'no'. They need to train themselves to express their wishes with precision. They need to touch objectivity. TWOs find action easier than contemplation, but the balance of action and contemplation redeems them from the compulsive side of their gift. They have to keep guarding their motives and freeing themselves from their compulsions in the shape of a Messiah complex or a relationship addiction. They have to come to understand that their giving has been an investment. When a TWO cries tears of self-knowledge, then redemption is near. They need to experience unconditional love.

TWOs are helped towards integration if they can recognise God

They can readily express emotion.

as the source of all compassion. They need to know God as the real lover of the world and of themselves. Our puny love can only be transformative when it takes its source from that unending love.

Humility is based on a genuine self-appraisal, including acknowledging their strategies of deceit and selfishness. At this point their autonomy is no longer an act of defiance, but is replaced by the realisation that they have found their identity in their true self – and therefore in God.

Initially they were proud of themselves and the value of the service they gave to others. From believing they could save the world, they now acknowledge their own limitations and personal needs. They no longer rescue people against their will. They begin to see there is no way to earn God's love, that even endless service can't deliver this love – it is always a free gift. The compassion of the TWO must also come from this same realisation. It is only this grace, God's love, that makes them lovable and gives them meaning and worth.

They are called to believe in God's grace to make them trust in their own ability to serve. When they accept God's unconditional love, they can stop craving approval.

TWOs need to take on the positive aspects of the energies familiar to the FOUR personality. These will help them to:

- make real contact with their own feelings and move on to acknowledge personal needs.
- grow to appreciate that they are lovable in their own right, irrespective of the services they render.
- learn that love is for the having – it cannot be bought.
- come to appreciate their real value and accept that they do not have to gain approval by being helpful – or helpless.
- begin to assist others without ulterior motives. They will no longer expect favours or expressions of gratitude.

The Giver: Symbols and Invitation

Here we highlight appropriate symbols for the TWO personality.

Animal: Dog
The dog, our favourite pet, is intent on pleasing its owner. It is affectionate and protective and will generously respond to approval. It enjoys being petted and given treats. Friendship with people seems to be the reason for its existence. The dog is sensitive and listening, a faithful defender of property. They are often uncomfortable with violence or hostility while having a real need for appreciation and love. Attention seeking, they can also be possessive and jealous.

The person who wears this skin will always manifest the desire to help. They need to be needed and love to fall in love. They are breathlessly persistent and inquisitive, and will often communicate by questioning.

Country: Italy
The land of the TWO is Italy. We are of course skirting here the realm of caricature, but the all-powerful Italian mama who manipulates her family offers us a distinctive image. The Italian portrait also hints at an excessive demonstration of caring and concern. There is attention and solicitude, but sometimes it will inevitably be carried too far. Italy also has an amazing fascination with bones, displayed at times in ecclesiastical settings, in dutiful searching and veneration for the remains of saints.

Colour: Red is the symbolic colour of the TWO. It is the colour of the warm heart, of love and intensity. Redeemed TWOs are capable of providing a warm heart without strings attached. As they move towards integration they become capable of opening to whatever love others may choose to offer and of responding to it with gratitude and as a gift.

Beliefs
- Others' needs are much more important than mine.
- It's they who need to be happy if I'm going to be loved.

Queries
- Will I be liked?
- Do they really love me?

Childhood message: TWOs come to the conclusion that they are loved because they are pleasing others. They may have needed to take care of their parents emotionally. The young TWO's sense of self could have developed from the way they perceived reactions or their overwhelming conviction that a great deal was required of them personally. They concluded that they could get what they wanted primarily by becoming indispensable.

Invitation: Towards true freedom

This freedom for the TWO personality ends the games of manipulation and bogus love. A sign that they are achieving this grace comes as they respond with gratitude. Liberated TWOs begin to set other people free. They move from pride towards humility.

As they acknowledge their own limitations and needs, they come to the realisation they have no need to save everybody, that love cannot be earned – neither God's nor anyone else's. All true love is unconditional. They start to accept themselves as worthwhile, irrespective of how helpful they may be to others. They then acknowledge their need to be loved in their own right and they abandon their excessive determination to help at all costs.

To move towards this freedom, TWOs often need to discover a place of silence and objectivity where they can begin to make friends with themselves, consider the facts about their own involvements, watch their motives and become more detached. They have to learn to say 'no' and to formulate their own needs. They will then practise doing good without attention and rewards.

Jesus as the servant of others

See Appendix 2: The Nine Enlightenments.

TWOs appreciate Jesus as a model of their own desire to be helpful to others. Jesus sees himself as sent by God to help and to save. As shepherd he seeks out the lost sheep and he calls on his disciples to do the same. He urges them to take the initiative in searching out the needs of others. TWOs readily see themselves in this light.

But precisely because gospel values emphasise the importance of being of service to others, TWOs may have considerable difficulty in recognising their compulsion for the vice it really is. Jesus is the giver without compulsion. He stressed the role of the giver to the point of disregarding religious laws when they prevent others from being looked after. All laws, he insisted, should be at the service of people.

With their longing to be helpful, TWOs can easily operate out of their compulsion to form a relationship which makes the other person dependent on them. They cling in their endeavour to be of personal service. They need to be needed. They can become the helpless helper and settle for appreciation. This was not the way of Jesus. The main drive behind his giving was compassion. He was not compelled by a hidden need to buy God's love.

Jesus demonstrates that real love is never won, neither from others nor from God. Love is always a free gift. Love is something given by choice. The gospel message is that God freely chooses to love. Human beings do not win this love by their actions: we are lovable for what we are and not for what we do. TWOs have to learn to live this faith in God's love. All love is ultimately communion rather than acts of service.

Along with their seeking to win love from others by taking pains to please them, TWOs, as we have seen, avoid acknowledging their own personal needs. They have to learn to love themselves enough to recognise that they cannot always be thinking only of the needs of others. Before he washed the feet of his disciples, Jesus allowed a woman to anoint his feet with expensive perfume and to wipe them with her hair.

TWOs may need some solitute to reflect on their relationships and in the silence give God's light the opportunity to penetrate their lives. This is what Jesus did. He perceived and acknowledged his own needs. After spending time with people, he would withdraw and recover his energies through dialogue with God. He was reluctant to tie people down. Even after working a miracle, he would sometimes send individuals away. Often he tells them not say anything to others.

The gospel encounter with Jesus will help TWOs to guard against:

- giving out of the need to feel good about themselves. Jesus calls for well-motivated, humble service.
- feeling guilty when they have personal needs. Jesus showed his own need and fears to his disciples and asked for their support.
- being unable to handle rejection. Through his own example, Jesus shows how this can be done.
- being too ready to volunteer. Jesus set limits and prayer structures for himself.

Jesus shows TWOs how to rejoice in:

- the fact that they are genuinely loving people. Jesus constantly demonstrates his ability to respond to need and not just to what is deserved.
- their natural ability to be gentle and non-threatening. The gospel highlights Jesus relating to children.
- the fact that they are generous, supportive and selfless. Jesus is willing to postpone his own rest in order to respond to the needs of others.
- their ability to show genuine concern for the individual. The gospel records, for example, how Jesus picks out Zacchaeus from the crowd.
- an ability to show true appreciation, as Jesus did to the centurion.
- a sensitivity to the emotional atmosphere around them. Jesus was conscious, for example, of the strain among his disciples and responded to it objectively.

Spur: To move towards personal freedom – seeing themselves as special and unique – and to join in the liberation of others.

Way of prayer for The Giver

See Appendix 3: Prayer and the Enneagram.

TWOs see life in terms of the services they can do for others. They keep connected by helping. Communal by nature, to reach deep prayer they have to resist the pull of the external and move inwards. They have to face the terror of not serving others. Only then can they discover for themselves the peace and energy which reside within. In this way they recover their balance. TWOs can be fearful of being alone. In prayer they learn how to replace goal-setting by God-dwelling.

Blind often to their own needs, TWOs may initially be required to find support and solace among family, friends or community. As they start ministering to themselves in this way – we have seen how it requires humility to do so – relationships become mutual and more healthy.

The inner journey can be hard for the TWO. Solitude is experienced as difficult. Self-intimacy often goes untried because of their habit of over-engagement in the external world. But God reveals himself to them as dwelling in the depths of their heart. They have to hear his still, small voice. They are called to become acquainted with what is going on within. This inner journey requires trust and spontaneity. They must become relaxed enough to follow their intuitions, their feelings and desires.

TWOs need to carve out some 'own time' for themselves, when they can relax without needing to be doing or helping. Even in prayer they will be tempted to assist God rather than hand themselves over.

In their meditation TWOs can bask emotionally in God and find freedom for self-expression. Their fears, frustrations and longings can be perfectly valid themes for their prayer. Their self-identity has to emerge from within where they can be alive and adrift on emotion. TWOs can make creative use of their distractions. They have to find trust in their own feelings and eventually in their own decisions.

TWOs must face and explore their pride. They have to reflect in particular on the relationships in their lives and decide what needs to change.

When they at last submit to determined inner work, allowing their lives to unfold, they learn, often to their surprise, how the interior world can nourish them. As they face their wounds, naming and handing over their personal needs, they find in God their ultimate source of healing and renewal.

The TWO route to well-being

Unhealthy characteristics: domineering, manipulative, self-serving
Average characteristics: possessive, friendly, self-important
Redeemed characteristics: caring, unselfish, warm, compassionate
Values: family, relationships, feelings, appreciation
Time tendency: past/future
Strongest sense: touch
Emotion least controlled: anxiety
Domination: identity
Masks: flattery, seduction, ambition
Problems: independence, loneliness

The TWO surrenders

- I no longer demand that others should feel guilty for not responding to my needs.

They need to appreciate that they are lovable in their own right.

- I let go of the abuse of food and medication to make up for my loneliness.
- I abandon the tendency to flatter others in order to make them feel good about me.

The TWO affirmations

- I affirm that my own happiness does not depend on pleasing others.
- I say 'yes' to others without expecting anything in return.
- I now affirm that I am lovable for who I am, not for what I do.

Pilgrim path for the TWO personality

The Giver's route of attachment

Each of the Enneagram pilgrim paths can move us through to the crux of the Christian message – our affinity with Christ and a universal encounter through the sharing of love.

The way of the TWO personality is the route of attachment, friendship or relationship. In spiritual terms, the pivotal point of all reality is relationship – Father, Son and Spirit. The Spirit flows from the relationship of Father and Son. The Incarnation, when Christ became man, has plunged the entire human race into this reality.

TWOs have to strive for a detached love. This will break down need and manipulation. They have to journey in order to rid themselves of the ties of security, esteem and importance. Moving away from power and prestige can entail a path of humiliation and suffering. They reach deliverance when in the end they stand alone.

This pilgrimage takes TWOs away from their attachments, away from co-dependency, and back to their own centre. Only here can they find their own identity and true enlightenment.

The gift of the TWO comes close to vulnerability and a willingness to share the rhythm and secrets of the heart. In this mysterious terrain of caring, empathy and true love so many of us stand in need. Without the gift of the TWO we will never be open enough for a God who longs for relationship. We all have to borrow from this vulnerability. This is the key to take us past our objectivity, our rules, our self-will, our addictions and our theologies. When we have it, and in so far as we have it, we can fall in love.

God image

As the TWOs move along their path of enlightenment, they stop trying to persuade God to conform to their own image of selfless love. The reality is that there is no need for persuasion: God is love. The heart of the journey is submission.

When you meet a TWO

- Tell them directly they don't need to be helpful in order for you to like them.
- Encourage them to talk about themselves. Ask them what they need. Don't let them focus only on you.
- Express a true appreciation of what they do.
- Remember, they work best in a group. Keep the lines of communication up and running.
- Let them know when they can help you best by not helping you at all.
- Be direct and genuine. They are likely to cut out when you are insincere.

The Achiever

7

FACE THREE
The Achiever

Performer, Animator, Status Seeker, Charmer, Director, Champion, Hustler, Communicator, Prime Mover and Role Model

We would rather be ruined than changed. We would rather die in our dread than climb the cross of the moment and see our illusions die.

W. H. Auden

My way: Seeking to achieve
My statement: 'I am successful.'
My centre: Heart
My passion: Deceit
My compulsion: Efficiency
My fear: Failure
My avoidance: Failure
My method: Image
My need: To see through the image
My virtue: Truth

Gift

The gift of the THREE personality inclines them to be confident, ambitious and successful. They are energetic and capable promoters. Keen to improve themselves, they work hard and are good motivators. By their style and enthusiasm they inspire others to excellence and success. They enjoy a challenge and focus on winning. They present themselves and their projects in a compelling way.

THREEs as children find reward in being busy and successful. They begin to compete and test out routes to success. They may discover that this earns them approval from the people nearest to them. Love and acceptance seems to depend on their achievements and they determine not to disappoint. Performance is valued more than involvement with people. They pursue what it is that will bring them success, neglecting their feelings and emotions in the process as they over-identify with their accomplishments.

THREEs develop a natural efficiency and enthusiasm for the task in hand. Their ability to get things done is attractive to others. They are imaginative, creative, productive and competitive. They are naturally energetic, good organisers and have a keen eye for detail. They plan for the future.

They have a busy social life and court popularity. There is danger that arising from their need to be successful, they can lose contact with who they are and identify only with their role and accomplishments.

THREEs are natural image makers. They are frequently opportunistic and workaholics. They can wear a mask and thrive on hustle and bustle. Often demanding taskmasters, and uncompromising with inefficiency and incompetence, they are reluctant to allow feelings to get in the way of success. They live their lives next to a timesheet. They like to direct projects and are reluctant to acknowledge how much they depend on other people. They can readily become exploitative, with scant regard for the truth.

They are lively conversationalists and are always able to produce or simulate a busy performance. Getting ahead is important. Since image is also vital to the success of their projects, they often dress with style and acquire other trappings that speak their success. They work hard but they like to make their strenuous efforts look easy and natural.

They live constantly behind a mask and learn to switch their feelings on or off according to requirements. They are never comfortable revealing their deeper selves and will readily divert attention to some undertaking of the moment if there is a danger that their feelings will be exposed.

When faced with failure they are inclined to withdraw and they can end up in despair. They are reluctant to look the bogus in the eye. They feed their energy from their most acclaimed successes.

THREEs will be inclined to say 'yes' to most of the following statements:

- I identify with professionalism and getting the job done.
- I like progress charts and other measures of achievement.
- I enjoy promoting myself and my projects.
- I hate to be told something I'm doing isn't producing results.
- I enlist others in order to achieve what I want.
- I believe that appearances count a good deal.
- Success is important and I set out to impress others.

'I am successful.'

- I like to keep myself on the go.
- It's not my style to let people in too close.
- I have no real problem when it comes to making decisions.

Challenges confronting The Achiever

THREEs have grown used to being praised for their accomplishments. Their performance and image have been rewarded rather than their emotional connections. They absorb the gospel of achievement and they may be driven by a neurotic need to succeed.

They have always been prepared to work hard for recognition. Willing and ready to take on leadership roles, they are only happy when playing to win. They are convinced that only winners merit love. They can use activity to avoid intimacy.

THREEs are capable of overestimating themselves. They may absorb their own successes to such an extent that they come to believe that most things they touch are significant and praiseworthy.

They will go through enormous pains to create an image that looks attractive. This pressure to take on the mantle of success leads them to their capital blindness – deceit. In order to succeed – or to be seen to succeed – THREEs are often tempted to reinvent the ground rules, reality or even the truth. They can deceive themselves into believing that a lie is the truth and they possess the ability to make others see it the same way. Deceit, and especially self-deceit, is at the heart of their dilemma.

Looking self-confident comes naturally to the THREE. That's why we readily trust them. They make persuasive sales people. First they sell themselves – we appreciate how competent they look – and we succumb to their charm and smooth plausibility. Because they are primarily interested in what works, they can be superficial. The inconsequential can be far more important than the substance. They are attached to the external – the image and the packaging – so that substance and the essentials are downgraded.

THREEs are apt to live outside themselves. They are spectators of their own performance. They enjoy an audience and can make the most of their acting talent. They stay so busy they seldom have time to be despondent. Even in relationships THREEs aim at efficiency.

They move swiftly from an idea into action and can bring great commitment to the task in hand. There is seldom scope for real feelings to surface. Personal life is not allowed to get in the way of the work schedule.

They have poor access to personal feelings. Emotions may have been on hold for years in the interest of effective job performance. Value depends on what is achieved and there is no place for those who fail to match up. It is traumatic for them to confront failure. They will avoid even the suspicion of failure like the plague.

THREEs are challenged to stop falling in love with their own show and to attend to their awry sense of self-worth. In the past they may have been mesmerised by what they have crafted themselves to be, but as they move beyond image and towards real health, they begin to look their self-deception in the eye and opt for depth. This is in no sense an easy journey for them to make. They have to face up to the challenge to quest inside for their own deep longing for unconditional love. This may be buried under a thousand hollow victories. But the search begins to free them from their need for applause and they can move at last towards the acceptance of God's wholly unmerited largesse and grace.

Hooks of the THREE

- Identifying with achievement and efficiency.
- Being competitive and avoiding failure at any cost.
- Judging people by their productivity rather than for who they are.

Route of integration for The Achiever

See Appendix 1: The Conversion Enterprise.

A fully redeemed THREE personality has somehow hacked his or her way to the truth, cutting through vanity, outer packaging and the image. This can be a painful enterprise.

THREEs discover the way to truth – their real gift – only when they embrace self-knowledge and finally refuse to accept their own inclination to deceive. To do this they may need to curb their search for success and find some space and stillness, a refuge where attainment is not ranked and where applause or admiration is unavailable.

Redeemed THREEs assist groups or communities to organise themselves so that society's deceits are named. They can share their talent for exposing the truth in its real perspective.

As we have seen, the trap for the THREE is their belief that to be efficient is to be worthy. Life, they insist, consists of achievements in competition with others. They are always searching for a quicker and more profitable way of doing things. Their aim is to be ahead of the field and they use time and those in partnership with them for this purpose. But the integration process, which will demand that they look at their own superficiality, sharpen their conscience and drop the restless quest for approval, urges them to put their competence and genuine gifts at the service of others.

Facing failure is traumatic.

They will then be able to widen their sphere of involvement and motivate others to discover their own gifts and potential.

Conversion comes for them when they can abandon themselves and their enterprises for a wider perspective (community) and for higher values (God), recognising then that the cosmos and the Kingdom have ultimate significance and meaning. Through this style of surrender they can offer their lives to God's action plan. They begin to see that a failure in their own projects is not necessarily a failure in God's plans. When THREEs embrace the whole world as God's Kingdom and begin to see their own limited role in perspective, they can rejoice in the accomplishment of others who are then no longer viewed or treated as competitors.

THREEs, as they move towards redemption, will take on the positive aspects of the SIX. These will help them to:

- struggle to develop the virtues of truth and honesty. They will drop the outward show and persistent efforts to impress others.
- begin to see through themselves and learn to acknowledge that substance is often more important than appearance.
- see their achievements in perspective. As they take stock of their accomplishments, they will also sense the real value of relationships and emotions.
- start to co-operate rather than compete with those around them. They see through their own determination to be top dog. They open up and acknowledge the feelings of others.
- acknowledge their own failures and understand that human frailty makes them less suspect and more acceptable.

The Achiever: Symbols and Invitation

The symbols can be helpful pointers to the underlying energies expressed by the personality types. Here we look at the Achiever, using two different animals to describe one energy.

Animal: Beaver/Peacock

Both these animals acquire their fame through use of their tail. The beaver, industrious and independent, uses its tail for hard work and creative enterprise. The beaver creates its own environment and has a pressing need for privacy. Efficiency is the goal of beaver life. By contrast, the peacock uses its tail to attract attention and achieve success through appearance. The peacock, notoriously vain, struts about showing off its beautiful tail-feathers. The person blessed with peacock feathers is usually gifted with the powers of conversation and persuasion. Both animals highlight the ethic of success.

THREEs are inclined to play the role that brings them most acclaim. Just as the peacock exhibits to best effect, THREEs enjoy parading in their finery in every aspect of their lives. They share a compulsive sense of responsibility and a commitment to education. They may be natural musicians.

Country: USA and England

The United States owes the wealth of its farmlands to the endeavour of the beaver and is the expression of beaver energy. The United States is the land of hard work, enterprise, efficiency and order. THREEs in the United States make it up the ladder. England, on the other hand, symbolises the realm of the peacock, sustaining its monarchy and apparently incapable of abandoning its House of Lords. The shoulder-to-shoulder stance of these two allies is based on a shared belief and commitment to competition and success. THREEs are rewarded by the capitalist system which puts so much emphasis on success. The packaging may be impressive but the content light.

Colour: Yellow is the symbolic colour of the THREE. It is a colour that cannot be denied or ignored. In a high-quality yellow, there is often an element of the dynamic. Like the colour yellow, THREEs stand out in a crowd, especially when healed and redeemed of their compulsion. A muddied yellow, on the other hand, often appears flash, sick or plain ugly.

Beliefs

- I am what I do and what I achieve.
- My value depends on the amount I achieve.

Queries

- Am I seen to be successful?
- What do I need to do to add to this image?
- Do people approve of my status and achievements?

Childhood message: From an early age THREEs are likely to have been given rewards and approval for their achievements. Success in competitive situations was probably acknowledged. Image was acclaimed rather than emotional sincerity.

Invitation: Towards truthfulness

Conversion for the THREE involves moving away from deceit towards truth. As long as they are stuck in the quest for competitive triumphs over others growth is limited. THREEs have to learn to see their momentary failures in context. They have to encounter self-critically their own dishonesty and compulsion to win. They need to face their own longing for love.

Integration brings truth and a more universal hope. Their own self-importance gives way to a broader concern for the common good and the improvement of society. Manipulation and subterfuge are replaced by values such as interdependence and mutual helpfulness.

Redeemed THREEs have found hope. They begin to empathise with the wider picture and move beyond a restricted self-interest. THREEs have to struggle to go deeper. They have grown accustomed to discounting feelings in case they interfere with efficiency and organisation. Caught up in their strivings for achievement, and the projects most likely to bring this about, their inner world can wither.

The route towards depth for the THREE demands patience and a willingness to experience emptiness and non-approval.

Jesus as the achiever

See Appendix 2: The Nine Enlightenments.

Jesus wanted passionately to succeed in the task he set himself. This is a goal orientation that THREEs find attractive. Jesus had seen at first hand the success of the mission triggered by the prophet John the Baptist, when people flocked to the Jordan to hear John's preaching. After his baptism, Jesus felt confident he could develop and use his gifts to urge on the coming of the Kingdom. But he always knew that Kingdom values were no guarantee of success.

To support his mission, Jesus developed his gifts of leadership. He worked hard at being a salesman of the Kingdom. He made himself available to people and learned how to hold their attention. As a communicator he could captivate large crowds. He told stories and parables, challenging people to make up their own minds. To achieve success he knew he had to make an impression. He was convinced of the truth and value of God's promises. He was prepared to support his appeal with miracles.

As an effective messenger, Jesus knew how to choose and train his co-workers. He looked for commitment from them and in return gave them positions of responsibility in his Kingdom work. He delegated part of his task as preacher and teacher.

As people with the single-minded goal of achievement in their lives, THREEs will find in Jesus an inspiring model. However, though Jesus lived for the success of his mission, he never viewed failure as the ultimate evil. He warned his followers that failure would be the cost of discipleship.

Driven by the search for success, THREEs run the risk of repressing their fears and their affections. They can readily find themselves out of touch with everyday life and blind to suffering around them. The gospel story demonstrates how Jesus avoided these temptations. He enjoyed the company of his followers – both men and women – giving most of his time to this close group. He shared with them his life, his insights and his goals.

It was a direct result of the success of his preaching and the power of his miracles that led many activists to want to make

Jesus king of Israel. But he turned his back on this path. Free of the compulsion of success at all costs, he knew the victory he promised would come paradoxically through failure and defeat. He became increasingly aware that for him personally the crown of the Kingdom would come through death on the cross.

The gospel encounter with Jesus will help THREEs to guard against:

- their hook of striving for total success at all costs. Jesus was rejected at Nazareth – the first of many rejections.
- spending too much time with external, image-making involvements. THREEs are proud of their accomplishments and their influence, but Jesus invites us all to humble service.
- their tendency to smooth-finish every project and to over-sell. Jesus calls us to live by the truth.
- being superficial, aggressive and vain. Jesus urges us to curb our deceit and be gentle and humble of heart.
- being too competitive. Jesus instructs his disciples not to claim titles such as rabbi or teacher, but to give of their best in the spirit of communal support.

Jesus shows THREEs how to rejoice in:

- their ability to set personal goals, appraise tasks and make decisions quickly. Jesus perceives the distress of the crowds. He chooses the Twelve after praying and sends them away to minister.
- a natural talent for good administration coupled with effective organisational skills. Jesus calls on his followers to be faithful servants and to make the most of their gifts.
- the positive use of their driving force and ability to persuade and lead others. Jesus reminds his disciples that it is God who is working through them.
- the part they can play in building up community. From a chance encounter Jesus brings enlightenment to the house of Zacchaeus the tax collector. He invites us all to be a transforming presence in our world.
- their confidence, but at the same time he calls us to a childlike trust in God.

Spur: To see through their own image-making and embrace the deeper truths.

Way of prayer for The Achiever

See Appendix 3: Prayer and the Enneagram.

THREEs are inclined to see life above all as a task that needs to be accomplished. Even in ministry, they can be caught up in the image of efficiency and success. But prayer is more about presence than productivity, about lingering creatively more than assessing or attracting achievement.

Often out of touch with their own feelings, THREEs can regard their emotions as a block to efficiency. But it is possible for them to recover their best energies and tap into their emotions in the quiet that goes with prayer.

Community and shared prayer can witness to the THREE that God's spirit is alive. But because they find it difficult to anchor themselves in the silence and centre of their hearts, they need to prepare by slowing down and opening deliberately to this world within. They are not easily engaged by this realm. THREEs have been accustomed to adopting the styles and attitudes of those making the running in society. Prayer is going to call them to some solitude.

Concentration and physical focus in the form of yoga postures, for example, may be helpful to them. Music, dance and drama can also form part of this preparation. In prayer they begin to go beyond outward image and what seems opportune.

Although prayer invites THREEs to a new experience of energy, they must allow their need for the functional, and for evaluation and all duplicity to dip away as scope is afforded to some stillness and spontaneity. Even in prayer, there is likely to be a strong temptation towards success. Again, the agenda is internal. The subject of their meditations may be their ambitions, their anxieties or their joys. These feelings should be attended to because this is not just introspection. They have to contemplate their own emerging imagery. This will take them inside and hold them. God and the person praying need to be in the prayer together.

THREEs must allow themselves to be set free by this spontaneous prayer. It takes them deeper than self-advertisement. The apparent time-wasting of prayer gives God the chance to attend to the quality of our love. The encounter is no longer defined by how good we look or who we know.

For the THREE, true freedom consists in holding one's ground, questing after lasting values and touching the genuine within. God has to burst through duplicity and image-making. It is in prayer that the mask drops and self-sufficiency is revealed as hopelessly inadequate. Applause ultimately is exchanged for love.

Deceit runs deep and is seldom healed at a canter. THREEs will always experience difficulty in praying the pain of failure. In meditation they may be able to use the Ignatian route of imagination, slipping into a scene created through a set text. This can prove a natural and meaningful way to encounter.

The THREE route to well-being

Unhealthy characteristics: deceptive, opportunistic, exploitative
Average characteristics: pragmatic, status-conscious, efficient
Redeemed characteristics: truthful, authentic, high-minded, energetic
Values: efficiency, status, identity
Time tendency: future/past
Strongest senses: touch, taste
Emotion least controlled: anxiety
Domination: image
Masks: vanity, prestige, security
Problems: insecurity, identity

The THREE surrenders

- I no longer demand that my grand expectations of myself should be fulfilled.
- I let go of my use of arrogance to make up for my own insecurity.

- I abandon the need to shut off my feelings in order to function.

The THREE affirmations

- I affirm that I am genuinely responsible to those who look up to me.
- I say 'yes' to the accomplishments and success of others.
- I now affirm that I have value irrespective of my achievements.

Pilgrim path for the THREE personality

The Achiever's route of endeavour

THREEs in the Enneagram system have a God-given ability to get things done. They love to make things happen. With this hunger for achievement goes the drive to attract other people into their enterprises. They are always on the lookout for new tasks, for new accomplishments.

'I couldn't have done it without you.'

In our day-to-day world of work, THREEs have an essential role to play. They travel the route of impressive engagement. THREEs are directly attracted to this world, and as they become involved themselves, they open up pathways for the rest of us. They see what needs to be done and they have what it takes to turn communal enterprise into successes. They are the matadors of the business world, of commerce, industry, politics and of our consumer society in general.

THREEs set most of the world's targets and then organise their achievement. If what we long for is what we become, THREEs must work to refine their engagements. We have seen how they are constantly tempted to fabricate their image. They are the master jugglers, the stylish captains of action and image. Most of us would settle to juggle two, three, perhaps four balls. Not so with the hungry achievers. With seven balls in the air they are looking for the eighth – and most of the time, after a fashion, they can find it.

But this is why they battle with deceit. Keeping eight balls in the air is likely to be a trick. To keep their show on the road, THREEs will be tempted to enter – or even invent – their own world of make-believe. Then nothing will be quite what it seems.

There is a danger here that the realm of accolades and multifarious accomplishments, successes and trophies will preclude any in-depth search for truth. As superficiality takes over, and enraptured by their own success, THREEs find themselves involved in endless and skilled performance. Any real attempt on the inner journey is at best likely to be postponed.

A pilgrim path based on deceit and precluding truth can only lead to a dead end. This is why the spiritual journey of the THREE has to involve silence and solitude, abandonment of the sales pitch – at least for a while. God finds space only when the excessive need to accomplish more has been stilled.

Deep prayer or contemplation can be defined as surrendering to the awareness that God loves us unconditionally. This is what the redeemed THREE has to come to. Then at last they can drop their illusion that there isn't enough love to go around. This realisation highlights for them the futility of their endless chase for acclaim.

The path of redemption for the THREE has to aim for integrity, for the true and the moral. If the THREE achieves this conversion, if they can make the connections that give them depth, their gift to the rest of us is precious indeed. Then they are set free to lead us into the highest endeavours. Eventually the enterprise of the THREE can be the gateway for the universal; in Christian terms, nothing less than a route to the Kingdom.

God image

As THREEs move along this path they stop seeing God as a master designer, the foreman, the ultimate achiever. Eventually, they will discover the unconditional God who wants nothing from them other than themselves.

When you meet a THREE

- Try to encourage them to get in touch with and express what they are really feeling.
- If you are trying to motivate them to do something, emphasise how it will help them to attain better results.
- If you feel you are being pushed into something or dragged along, make your protest. They're likely to be oblivious to the fact that you are hurting. Let them know.
- Try not to take it too badly when their attention span begins to wander and they look as though they are about to blank you out entirely.
- Remember, they don't find it easy to accept that they are valued in their own right. They may not look as though they need to be told this, but they do.

The Artist

8

FACE FOUR

The Artist

Individualist, Aristocrat, Dilettante, Special Person, Listener, Dreamer, Romantic, Melancholic, Stylist, Outsider, Aesthete and Unique Performer

Now let us do something beautiful for God.

Mother Teresa of Calcutta

My way: Seeking to create
My statement: 'I am unique.'
My centre: Heart
My passion: Envy
My compulsion: To be different
My fear: The ordinary
My avoidance: The mundane
My method: Creative expression
My need: Sense of reality
My virtue: Equanimity

Gift

The gift of the FOUR personality motivates them to seek out the unusual. They are creative and value authenticity. They are emotionally honest and sensitive. Their clothing and environment express their sense of uniqueness and their need for beauty and depth of meaning. They have a fundamental need to be special. They are idealistic and focus on relationships. They readily empathise with other people's sufferings, especially in moments of crisis.

FOURs see themselves as different. They have an expectation of being let down and can readily feel thwarted or offended. This inclination to sadness derives from their feeling of being special but misunderstood. They believe that nobody can possibly grasp their pain and loneliness.

As children they may have felt there was nobody there to comfort or support them. They sometimes decide to distance themselves from others before they are themselves rejected. They can avoid emotional involvement by resorting to an elaborate fantasy life.

FOURs may be artistic. They are usually sensitive to beauty, to mood and to the feelings of others. They can view their own artistic good taste as compensation for a lack of self-esteem. They are apt to rely on imagery and symbols to express their feelings. They have an unusual sense of style and dress and they may couple this with a tendency towards the eccentric and exotic. They have no time or relish for the ordinary and therefore find it difficult to live in the present.

FOURs tend to lurch between joy and sorrow, the tragic and the highly dramatic. This can become a well-worn way of escaping the ordinary. They believe in the uniqueness of their own feelings and can be disdainful of the feelings of others. They can be envious of what other people seem to possess.

FOUR personalities enjoy ritual and drama and can be theatrical in their responses. Manners and good taste are important to them. They long for originality and simplicity. They are often on the brink of the spontaneous but usually take refuge in elaborate rehearsal. Longing can be more important than having. Often they have to struggle with feelings of inferiority.

They believe that if they become too ordinary or down-to-earth, people would refuse to take them seriously. Because of their fear that others will not understand them, they tend to retreat into themselves and become melancholic and sad. On occasions they need to indulge this melancholia in order to feel in touch with real life.

They analyse a great deal and frequently dwell on the past. They can be self-absorbed, moody and subject to depression. They may sometimes direct their aggression against their own bodies.

FOURs can have elitist standards. They may be attracted to what is beyond their grasp, but should they achieve their objective, they can still be disappointed.

FOURs will be inclined to say 'yes' to most of the following statements:

- Sometimes people accuse me of being over-dramatic. But they don't really understand how I feel.
- I seem to be more bothered than most about the termination of relationships.
- I like to surround myself with beautiful things.
- Other people have difficulty understanding me.
- I like to do things properly and with some style.
- I am better face-to-face than in a group.
- I try to look casual and natural.
- I can be melancholic and often feel vulnerable.
- People sometimes think I regard myself as special.
- I think I am more sensitive and imaginative than most people.

'I am unique.'

Challenges confronting The Artist

Many FOURs are more at home with their art – which may be their very way of life – than they are with other people. FOURs long for a lost simplicity. As they struggle for authenticity, they are inclined to express their feelings indirectly through symbols or rituals. They do this, in part at least, in order to deal with the pain of loss and the fear of rejection. What they have to develop in the end is a genuine capacity to love. They have to drop their conviction that there is not enough love to go around.

FOURs are tempted to shape their lives as a work of art. Their immediate environment is important to them. We have to remember that the theatre, films and television are the natural domains of the FOUR. Clothes, decor, friends, hobbies and even the details of the daily round are collected together as if they were all elements in a stage performance. This is part of the FOURs search for authenticity. Nevertheless, FOURs can often be ill at ease with people and struggle with feelings of inferiority. They can come to regard imminent eclipse as their fate.

The capital blindness of the FOUR is envy. They can detect immediately – and will even be looking out for – those who rival them in style or talent. They will be aware of who has a cooler image and who is being more natural and imaginative. There is very little that a FOUR can't be imaginative about.

In relationships FOURs can express their envy in the form of jealousy. They make constant demands on love. They can live in fear that somebody will come on the scene who could turn out to be a more stylish companion.

FOURs detest the ordinary and can enjoy life on the edge. They are self-absorbed and spend long periods day-dreaming. Making comparisons turns them competitive. They may be capable of self-mockingly articulating their elitist strivings, their moodiness or their snobbishness, but moving into the realm of real self-criticism is more demanding. This may be true even if they have come to the point of realising that their eccentricity can be the reason for their failure to really love.

FOURs like to indulge in melancholia, feelings of regret and expressions of lamentation. The grass in the distance is always greener. They let the mood of melancholy crash down into what most of us would regard as deep depression. FOURs believe that the more they suffer, the more they deserve to be rescued. They can actually take pleasure from their sufferings. The greater the pain and the depression, the more creative FOURs can be. Their longing adds up to a claim on perfect love.

They will readily blow hot and cold towards their partners and the issue of self-esteem can be ever-present. They will query: 'Would I have been abandoned if I were more worthy?' There may be clear-cut avoidance of the moment. The present can easily be regarded as a rehearsal for the future. They may give considerable internal attention to preparation for the arrival of a future lover.

FOURs need to become aware of what may be contributing to their compulsive attraction to the unavailable. Keeping intimacy – and even life itself – at a safe distance is an art form for the FOUR.

FOURs are attracted to tragedy and to loss. They prefer the richness of melancholia to what others would describe as happiness. On the other hand, if abandonment threatens, they will resort to a telling list of emotional strategies and high dramas. They take their feelings and their inner life seriously and, when hurt, can be most aggrieved. FOURs are tempted to direct their aggression against themselves. An inclination to anorexia or bulimia can appear among FOUR women.

The FOUR personality is called to the realisation that their world-view of life and love as being in short supply is not standard, but stems from their own feelings of unworthiness. They are challenged to abandon this realm of ongoing emotional and spiritual deprivation and to put their trust in life's mystery and fullness. They have to stop clamouring after what they already possess – God's love.

Hooks of the FOUR

- Envy: 'Others have what I am missing.'
- Attachment to the mood of melancholy.
- The search for authenticity, which encourages the feeling that the present is not real.

Route of integration for The Artist

See Appendix 1: The Conversion Enterprise.

FOURs need to bring discipline into their lives. In particular, it is essential for them at times to distance themselves from their feelings and uncover their own sources of harmony.

They need to direct their longings towards obtainable ends. Reality is present in the ordinary. They have to overcome their compulsive attraction to the unavailable. Avoiding the extremes, they have to discipline themselves to live in the present and be on their guard against mood swings. It is important for them to keep dipping back into reality. A redeemed FOUR can deal with real life in the here and now. Dreaming about the future and wistful memories of the past need to be guarded against.

As they move towards integration, FOURs may have to open up to an early experience of loss in their lives. Their failure to grieve may be preventing the surge they long for towards liberation. It

Attachment to the mood of melancholy.

may be essential for them to acknowledge anger or the idealisation of someone who has exercised an undue influence. FOURs must also be willing to take a hard look at their elitist tendencies. Rather than comparing themselves with others, they have to accept their own gifts and be prepared to share them for the benefit of the wider community.

FOURs are capable of great depth of feeling. When they find the freedom to express in creative fashion their sense of the beautiful – and even the tragic – they can be a sensitive source of service and the creators of real works of art. They often have a gift, for example, for understanding and supporting people who are in emotional turmoil. Drawing on their own experience of suffering, they can face the fears and dreads of others and help them through their darkness. FOURs have a capacity for supporting people through long periods of recovery.

Balance and equanimity for the FOUR resolves the suffering caused by being pulled towards the unobtainable and repelled by what is familiar or close at hand. This brings to awareness the liberating recognition that it is possible to possess just enough of what is really needed.

FOURs experience this point of balance when they can quietly return their awareness to the present moment and pay respect to the pleasure of the 'enoughness' within their grasp. Appreciation and gratitude for what they already possess can be a constant resource. They need to recognise how they give selective attention to negative aspects of the present situation.

To bring about integration FOURs need to move towards the positive aspects of type ONE. This will enable them to:

- cut out envy and abandon the futile exercise of making comparisons.
- come into the present and accept the harsh aspects of ordinary life along with the good.
- distance themselves from their feelings at times and avoid being overwhelmed by negative feelings.
- stop working everything through in their imagination.
- use their gifts no matter how unimportant these may seem.

The Artist: Symbols and Invitation

The symbols highlighted in this section are intended as pertinent pointers to the major energies relating to the Enneagram types. Here we describe the FOUR.

Animal: Cat
The cat is an animal with class, an aristocratic pet. We attribute nine lives to the cat and historically it has shown remarkable resilience and determination to survive. The cat gives the impression of selecting its owner. It can be aloof and mysterious. The cat values its independence but needs people to prosper. It is highly curious, even philosophical. It will not respond by 'name', ignores all calls on obedience, and is particular about its diet. The cat is sensitive and delicate and these days finds a part to play in films, on TV and on stage. Ideally, these roles in keeping with the aspirations of the person who wears this skin, need to be melodramatic, special and unique.

Country: France
FOURs can readily delight in the style of France. This is their symbolic territory. France, historically, has been reluctant to integrate. It remains synonymous with independence. The French way is refined, stylish, some would say elitist. There is a relish here for haute cuisine and haute couture, for high fashion and the finest wines. The unusual is attractive. The FOUR naturally identifies with this penchant for the special.

Country: FOURs can readily delight in the style of France. This is their symbolic territory. France, historically, has been reluctant to integrate. The French way is refined, some would say elitist. They have a relish for haute cuisine and haute couture, for high fashion and the finest wines. The unusual is what attracts. The FOUR naturally identifies with this penchant for the special.

Colour: The symbolic colour of the FOUR is mauve or violet. This colour is in the purple range but cannot be specified exactly. It is subtle, mystical, melancholic and understated. This is the colour that mediates between red, representing the masculine, and blue, the feminine. The integrated FOUR stands for synthesis and balance. FOURs typically dress in this way – with exceptional good taste and often in a stylish dark colour.

Beliefs

- I have to be special.
- Others have what I want. I'm missing out.
- A special love will make me worthy.

Queries

- What do you think of me?
- Am I being loved enough?

Childhood message: FOURs may have a sense of abandonment or deprivation. They may also have been valued for identifying with the pain of one of the parents.

Invitation: Towards authenticity

FOURs are inclined towards the creative, artistic and romantic. They ultimately find authenticity on their way to union with God. They may need to confront the real experiences of loss in their lives, acknowledging perhaps the rage they feel towards the particular individuals involved.

They have to move on from making comparisons to looking critically at their own exaggerated sense of entitlement and share their real inner treasures with others. Change and conversion for the FOUR involves allowing themselves to journey from self-centred envy to a chastened composure. Seeing through their own need to be special and to gain attention, they begin to live their lives in a more sustained serenity. They can help redeem the world through their art, their appreciation of community and their longing for beauty. They are willing to endorse the highest values and they respond freely to the freshness of the moment. They no longer cling to the tragic or dramatic in their lives, they accept the way things are and find fulfilment in being drawn into the mystery of life – where God dwells.

Among the goals of the FOUR is the development of a grounded realism so they can direct their longings towards achievable goals. They need to keep their attention on the issues of the moment and accept reality even when it is unspectacular, lonely or grubby. This will begin to help them sort out the endless swinging between euphoria and depression. Then they can release their very personal and sensitive love with its unique range of feeling.

Jesus as the sensitive artist

See Appendix 2: The Nine Enlightenments.

Gospel stories show Jesus in the mode of the FOUR, being both sensitive and compassionate. He is counsellor of the afflicted, defender of the despised. Despite the cosmic dimension of his message, he is always interested in the individual at the level of the heart. He wanted his listeners to know that there is nothing more special than their relationship with God.

Jesus knew every human emotion. The gospel writers report how he openly acknowledged his sadness and was not ashamed of his tears. When he heard the news, for example, of the death of his friend Lazarus, the gospel tells us, 'He began to weep'.

In the characteristic way of the FOUR, Jesus made exceptional artistic use of symbols and drama. His everyday experience inspired him to create images, parables, even miracles, to emphasise his mission and to encourage his listeners to come to know the embrace of God's love.

He was the artist in touch with the banquet of life. He spent days in the mountains and in the deserts. The crowds shared his fame and his loneliness by the lakes. He chose the lifestyle of the storyteller. He was the parable-spinner who fashioned his own imaginative world from what he shared with his audience: the fishes netted, the fig tree, the mustard seed, the birds of the air, the lilies of the field, the leaven in the bread, the sheep and the goats, and the rains that fall alike on the just and the unjust. He was creating a new script that would challenge old fixations. He appealed to the imagination.

The core of Jesus' message – the coming of the Kingdom – was unwrapped in the same fascinating style. The symbol would highlight the message.

When Jesus entered the city of Jerusalem on an ass, and was hailed as Son of David, the messianic symbolism was not lost on the Jewish people. Unfortunately, they attempted to use his kingship for their own ends. But Jesus rejected this. He knew at first hand the withering impact of an over-strict affinity to the law. The traditional faith lacked heart and spirit, and was incapable of extending the freedom he longed to deliver.

Despite his artistry, Jesus' way of life was unaffected and natural. Openness characterised his style. He was unconcerned about the labels which would be attributed to him by his enemies because he associated with people who skirted the law.

Characteristic of the FOUR, Jesus' cosmic message continually bridged the gulf for his followers between the sacred and the profane. There was no separation. Everything was holy and all belonged to God.

FOURs instinctively know how to use melancholy to attract attention to themselves. Envy is also a tactic. It highlights the gap that lovers must attempt to fill. But Jesus refused this route. He never portrayed himself as a lone or tragic figure. He avoided self-pity. He knew there were people willing to persecute him, but he reminded his followers that they would be persecuted even more. As his enemies plotted to bring about his downfall, Jesus reacted by increasing the pace of his mission in the heart of Jerusalem.

In the same way, whenever Jesus spoke to his followers of his anticipated death, he added the prediction that he would rise again. He wanted to present his going as a victory rather than a tragedy. He never used pain as a claim on the world. He was too secure in his Father's love. The man of sorrows was ultimately a messenger of hope.

The gospel encounter with Jesus will help FOURs to guard against:

- their reluctance to be ordinary.
- the tendency to be envious and to complain.

- standing aloof and being snobbish, and espousing elitist causes. Jesus was comfortable with tax collectors and sinners, and they with him.
- allowing their fantasy life to keep them out of touch with reality.
- performing too often and hugging depression. Jesus continually gives thanks.
- being over-sensitive to criticism. Jesus is acceptant of rejection.

Jesus shows FOURs how to rejoice in:
- their appreciation of beauty in the world around them.
- an ability to express themselves artistically.
- their sensitivity to people and awareness of the emotional tone of a group. Jesus responded to Mary's sensitivity at the wedding feast of Cana.
- a natural ecumenism. They have no need to separate the sacred from the secular.

Spur: To move from feelings of futility, isolation and waste to being a self-possessed contributor to all that is sustaining, good and beautiful.

Way of prayer for the Artist

See Appendix 3: Prayer and the Enneagram.

FOURs are often comfortable centre stage. But in prayer they have to share the limelight with God! It is here they learn that nothing is ordinary in God's eyes.

Because relationships are important to the FOUR, shared prayer and liturgy can be a welcome route to encounter with God. They find the communal agenda and scope for spontaneity energising and supportive.

Other creative support forms can also work for the FOUR – yoga, massage and keeping a journal, writing up what is happening and developing in their lives in the here and now. The journal will also help to keep these feelings in perspective. It can be a good safety valve for externalising inner issues. In the same way, charismatic prayer, drama, music, singing and poetry can be effective introductions, and much suited to the interests and talents of the FOUR.

Living from within and awash as they often are with feelings, FOURs are tempted to give exaggerated importance to the fullness of their heart. However, when centred, they are more aware of the influx of their emotions and can turn them to positive use.

The FOUR personality's self-presentation as special and different leads them to avoid simple joys and sorrows, but the giftedness of the FOUR is always enhanced by appreciation of the world around them. Nature and beauty, because of their essential truth, can also lead them into prayer. Because they have problems with issues relating to intimacy and possession, FOURs can make creative use of their dreams, using them to probe their own vibrant inner world.

Solitude can be troublesome when you fail to recognise your own inner powers. FOURs may find it difficult to anchor themselves in the silent centre of their hearts, but they need to discover the means of opening up this world within. They must find enthusiasm for this inner state and allow God to be there. This is how they will gain access to the source and meaning of their lives.

It is crucial for the FOUR to thank God for their own giftedness – their ability to create the beautiful. They should approve of all their creations with a prayer of gratitude. In this direct way they learn to value and acknowledge what it is they possess: creativity, sensitivity and the goodness and happiness they share with those around them.

Prayer can plunge FOURs back into the ordinary. Their prayer, to be wholehearted, needs to be expressive. Thoughts about relationships, feelings, anxieties, joys and sorrows, the future, everything caught up in their mood swings, can be the object of their meditations. They have to trust and dare to be themselves, attending to the leadings of the Spirit.

In particular they can hand over their self-concerns, their envies and jealousies. FOURs need to present their doubts. Demons need to be faced and named. They can pile up and place their lamentations before God. In this way prayer will fine-tune their gift of balance and put them at ease with the way things are.

The FOUR route to well-being

Unhealthy characteristics: self-hating, mournful, alienated
Average characteristics: romantic, melancholic, aesthetic
Redeemed characteristics: creative, sensitive, disciplined
Values: identity, relationships, performance, style
Time tendency: past
Strongest senses: touch, taste
Emotion least controlled: anxiety
Domination: image
Masks: sadness, competition, shame
Problems: independence, identity

The FOUR surrenders

- I no longer demand unrealistic accomplishments from myself or from others.

They need a sense of reality.

- I let go of my feelings of hopelessness and despair.
- I stop feeling shameful and abandoned by others.

The FOUR affirmations

- I affirm the goodness of my life, my friends and myself.
- I say 'yes' to the goodness and beauty I can bring to the world.
- I now affirm that I am not defined by my feelings.

Pilgrim path for the FOUR personality

The Artist's route of refinement

The journey of the FOUR personality in the Enneagram system can be described as the route of refinement. The artist searches for the way of the truly aesthetic. Here simplicity itself will reveal the priceless gem, the unparalleled art, the unrivalled truth. FOURs have an eye for whatever is beautiful. They long for the graceful and they suffer when the world fails to match their quest for excellence.

As we have seen, FOURs enjoy stylish surroundings, beautiful clothes and choice company. But this search and longing for the beautiful can also thwart and capture. This happens for them – as it does for all of us – when they overdo their gift. The quest for exclusivity then takes them beyond refinement and sets them adrift in a realm of eccentricity. FOURs will often be tempted to cut their losses and settle for this world. The danger is that in this quirky zone their inner journey will grind to an abrupt halt. Once again this is the land of the excessive – of too much colour (or too little), of too much jewellery, too much style, outlandish dress sense, of the egocentric splurge replacing the search for the truly beautiful.

Redeemed FOURs excel in the search for refined beauty, they focus on the tasteful, on what it is that distinguishes and uplifts. Here the realm of the extravagant and the self-obsessed has been relinquished. Now the search is for beauty in the ordinary, recognition and acceptance of the simple. They move towards taste and class. They are in touch with quality and style, with intense feelings and profound insights.

A vital consideration for the redeemed FOUR is the contribution they make. What is all this beauty for? They search for a satisfactory answer. They know they have to use their art – what it is that makes them different – for the benefit of the world. What FOURs possess they must give away. 'What is my most refined contribution?' This is a valid question and their response will often centre on bringing out the giftedness and specialisms of others.

FOURs need contemplation. They have to discover their true centre. Here the refined truth will be a simplification. They will learn to see through the superfluous, to surrender into their own spacious centre which in its emptiness contains all grace. It is the refined truth which is the greatest of all. Conversion calls for them to jettison their world of minimal love and to discover significance in shared beauty. The FOUR is esteemed, in common with all the world – precious in God's love.

God image

FOURs are attracted to the God of mystery and darkness – the God who is absent. There is power for the FOUR in the hidden. And God does hide. FOURs are also lured by the unobtainable. The absence can move them into fantasy and they must guard against being caught up in the unknown to the point where the longing for the chase blocks true discovery. There is a bitter-sweet feeling in absence which can curb true recognition. In the end, the FOUR – like all of us – has to submit to the proximity of God.

When you meet a FOUR

- Remember that the emotions they express are real. These may seem excessive, too dramatic, but don't try to talk them out of it.
- Let them know what you feel as well as what you think.
- Be straight when asking for their assistance. They may appear to be caught up in their own world but in reality they will be very happy to help.

- Remember, even if you don't suspect it, they may have low self-esteem. Let them see that you value them. Allow for their intuitions.
- Acknowledge their feelings. If they appear to be down or moody, ask them to share how they feel. Help them to stay focused on the present. You may be able to help them lighten the situation.
- Be happy to compliment them, especially for their creative and individual contribution.

The Observer

9

FACE FIVE

The Observer

Thinker, Analyst, Researcher, Specialist, Expert, Discoverer, Investigator, Boffin, Loner and Seeker

When you are detached from the world, you see everything coming from the hands of God, always fresh and beautiful. Everything is a symbol of God.

Bede Griffiths

My way: Observing
My statement: 'I am perceptive.'
My centre: Head
My passion: Greed
My compulsion: Knowledge
My fear: Meaninglessness
My avoidance: Emptiness
My method: Observation
My need: To be involved
My virtue: Detachment

Gift

The gift of the FIVE personality motivates them to seek understanding. Sensitive, objective and creative thinkers, they can mobilise their patience and self-sufficiency to assist others in times of stress. They become knowledgeable and develop unusual expertise. Because they are emotionally detached and can work independently, they are capable of making good decisions, perceive interrelated patterns and can produce original ideas.

As children FIVEs may have settled for the quiet life. They quickly develop the ability to retreat inside themselves. However, they remain watchful of what is going on around them. At an early age they may have experienced the people close to them as too intrusive or too distant and they opt for an emotional disengagement. They readily move into their own world of private thoughts.

FIVEs learn how to absorb information but are often reluctant to share it. They keep an eye on what is happening while developing the skill of melting into the crowd.

FIVEs have a gift for taking in the wider picture but they experience difficulty in becoming involved. They have an impersonal air and they are reluctant to share, fearing this will leave them drained. They find too much closeness exhausting.

They are spectators rather than players. They can be secretive and superior. They have learned how to shun the limelight. They can be stingy with themselves, their time and their money.

FIVEs also experience difficulty becoming emotionally engaged. They avoid concrete commitments. They are defensive of their own space and don't regard emotions as very important. They compartmentalise their lives and like to regard their home as their castle.

They will more readily tell you what they think than what they feel. Their direction is inward and in the interests of preservation they are careful about commitments generally and their emotional involvements in particular. They have learned how to minimise their needs.

FIVEs prefer to avoid social gatherings and lack skill at small talk. In a one-to-one situation they can be very receptive and non-judgemental. They acquire and hoard knowledge in order to avoid the feeling of emptiness.

Always keenly aware of what it is they don't know, FIVEs are reluctant to be found wanting. They try to avoid being the centre of attention. If they have a scientific leaning, they can readily become technical addicts. They can recoil from the details of practical living and prefer to blend in rather than stand out.

FIVEs will be inclined to say 'yes' to most of the following statements:

- I tend to keep my feelings to myself.
- I defend my private time and space.
- I distrust the people who have power over me.
- I have trouble reaching out or asking for what I need.
- I am good at rational thinking but I also have a lively fantasy life.
- If an issue comes up, I like to work it out for myself before discussing it with others.
- I fear that too many commitments will take away my energy.
- I can relate to silence more than most.
- I observe and try to make sense of what is happening.
- I try to see the wider picture rather than the detail.

'I am knowledgeable.'

Challenges confronting The Observer

FIVEs believe they can meet the demands of their world by acquiring as much data as possible. Knowledge for the FIVE is tantamount to power. But the information they collect is somehow never enough. They are challenged to probe for the impact and hidden significance of their capital blindness – covetousness.

As a defensive strategy, FIVEs often opt to withdraw. They are private people. They will journey far to search out information, but they are very reluctant to be searched. These types are not natural givers. They are inclined to hold on to their intellectual and material possessions and can be ingenious in defending their private space.

FIVEs will try to avoid emotional entanglement. They are often uncomfortable with feelings and relationships. They fear imminent invasion and work hard to minimise contact. Many of them are naturally inclined towards asceticism and celibacy. In their personal requirements they are usually quite modest, but this skimping can have an ulterior motive: it can feed the illusion that they are independent of others and minimise interaction.

FIVEs will sometimes be at pains to avoid precise commitments. They usually feel comfortable in a world of theory and ideas and will happily restrict themselves to chasing knowledge or understanding connections rather than engage in the world of social or political reality.

They like to divide their lives carefully into departments and are then at pains to defend the separate boundaries. These compartmentalised worlds – and even the people who inhabit them – are not encouraged to mix. This tactic protects them from emotional overstrain. In this sense they are stingy with others and with themselves. Financial dealing is not their scene. In open conflict situations they will usually lean back on intellectual arguments or opt for a hasty exit.

FIVEs are independent people. They can be happy with the hermit life and they refuse to be sidetracked by petty concerns. Their inclination is to search out the wider picture. They are prone to avarice and their love of privacy can turn into loneliness.

Because they have an inner sense of emptiness, they fear that if they give they will end up totally spent. They live with the constant fear of being sucked dry and may choose to seek protection in isolation. Their attempts to escape will often help to explain to themselves and to others the full agenda that the FIVE covertly seeks to retain. They may carry round with them a rather profound aura, but they usually have to dig deep to make contact with their own sense of inner worth.

Detachment is at once the gift and the obsession of the FIVE. Their disinterest in financial matters or material concerns is often a cause of frustration for those near to them. But they have a natural ability to absorb objectively what is going on around them.

They can bring the same skill to the listening process and are therefore gifted counsellors. The healthy FIVE, capable of insight and objectivity, can readily withdraw emotionally and assist others to come to terms with what for them may be utterly confusing.

But the real challenge facing the FIVE personality is to make sense of their feeling of personal scarcity. They have to come to terms with the possibility of sharing what they will initially regard as diminished resources. Tempted to conserve their time, affections, involvements and material goods, the FIVE has to risk the paradox that only by giving these away can they be enriched.

Hooks of the FIVE

- Privacy and avoiding the action.
- Feeling afraid to feel.
- Intellectual snobbery.

Route of integration for The Observer

See Appendix 1: The Conversion Enterprise.

The FIVE personality highlights the way in which an identical character trait – detachment – carries with it both a grace and a curse. FIVEs are drawn into the search for intellectual links and ultimately for wisdom. They are inclined to think before they act –

and to go on thinking. An essential life task for the FIVE is to embrace action and commitment.

For a redeemed FIVE the fruit of the spirit becomes detachment and objectivity. But unhealthy FIVEs usually have to discover their need to be involved and to take decisive action. They have to open up to the meaning of the Incarnation and its practical consequences. Learning to love, to allow in some passion, some rugged involvement, presents them with permanent challenges. They have to find a means of giving their energy away. They must also uncover for themselves enough trust to allow for mystery and the unfathomable.

All of us, as we tread the path of integration, have to move to some extent against the grain of our natural compulsion. FIVEs, the even-souled contemplatives, must overcome their fears and find the courage to abandon their role as observer in favour of commitment. They have to journey outwards into the unknown, the messy, even to the Cross.

They have to experience that knowledge comes through the

They often opt to withdraw.

heart and the senses as well as through the head. Avoiding the temptation to disengagement, they have to be inventive enough to find practical ways of sharing their insights. Only then will they learn in a concrete way how their giving leads to receiving.

It is essential for many FIVEs to be on their guard against snobbery, arrogance and conceit. Observers best discover the gift of authentic wisdom as they begin to cast off their search for privacy and their fear of being overwhelmed by external demands, and encounter purposefully the mystery and diversity of other people. As they move from seeing to acting and release their obsessive taking, FIVEs have the gifts to make valid and important connections, becoming sharp-eyed spiritual and political visionaries, researchers and teachers.

Meditation and prayer are important sources of power for the FIVE. Often, before they can break out beyond themselves into the redemptive world of action, they have to cultivate their own interior life. In practice this will mean replacing their longing for knowledge with an unquenchable longing for God. Only when they have discovered their ultimate security in God, will they be able to reach out without counting the cost.

To bring about conversion FIVEs need to embrace the best aspects of the EIGHT. This will help them to:

- move towards commitment and into the action. They need to journey from theory and observation into practical activity.
- begin to realise that self-knowledge is not restricted to analysis or confined to any theory. They will also become aware that emotions too are important.
- be able to share more of themselves as they begin to change. In order to offset their avarice and possessiveness, they need to find the courage to risk self-disclosure, becoming more generous in terms of sharing their knowledge, money and time.
- join more openly with others and bring trust to their relationships. They will experience the warmth of genuine friendship and be able to share emotionally at a deeper level.
- become more circumspect about their own hasty judgements and begin to give weight to the opinion of others.

The Observer: Symbols and Invitation

The symbols are intended as a gentle, descriptive portrait of the energies relating to the Enneagram types. Although emblematic, they can be remarkably accurate and instructive.

Animal: Owl
Symbol of wisdom, the owl sits remote, motionless and watching. The saucer-like eyes of the owl absorb the view. The owl will only swoop when it has its prey in sight. It is accurate, but even when successful in the kill, will eat only what is needed. The owl is noted for its invisibility, patience, wisdom and perception. The person who wears the owl skin is usually gifted with utmost patience and has a great capacity for enjoying their own company.

Country: Scotland
Sister Mary Helen Kelley suggests that Scotland is shrouded in the power of the Owl. Caricature certainly portrays Scotland as stingy, careful with money and monosyllabic in speech. The exclamation 'Hoot, man' tells the same story. The Scots also parade their plaids, a style of camouflage similar to the feathers of the owl, helping them to remain hidden.

Colour: The symbolic colour of the FIVE is deep blue. This represents the introverted, passive and receptive quality of the FIVE. This is the colour that stands for the feminine (Mary, the Mother of God). It is representative of the deepest levels of the subconscious. It also stands for contemplation.

Beliefs

- You can't trust emotions.
- Use logical thinking to work it out.
- In the end, you are on your own.

Queries

- Have I taken in enough information on this topic?
- Can I really trust this person?

Childhood message: Family in childhood was experienced as remote or intrusive. Withdrawal was a safety tactic. FIVEs coped with the isolation by developing detachment.

Invitation: Towards wisdom

The FIVE's strategy for security and survival is bolstered by moving towards their head and its carefully stockpiled knowledge. As long as they are stuck in this zone, their search for growth will be limited.

FIVEs readily seal off the emotions and withdraw into solitude. Life invites them to move in the opposite direction, towards commitment and action. They have to learn that it pays no dividends to cultivate their inner world unless they eventually engage in the tough reality of the outer world. They must move on from introspection to practical mission. Only then can they find repose and security in God who will lead them gently to the fullness of wisdom. The mystery at that stage no longer needs to be examined.

By getting involved in what is happening, and allowing life to be their teacher, they free themselves from their instinct to store and protect their own privacy. They can reach authentic wisdom if they move out from behind their defences and risk themselves in the encounter with other people. They begin to realise it is the community that rescues them from poverty. In this way their own giftedness is exposed.

FIVEs must practise expressing emotions directly. This is a style of giving that eventually helps to convince them that giving does not deplete, that it is in the profound act of releasing that space to receive more gifts from God is created. Then they can begin to shed the resources they have stored up against future eventualities. As they free themselves to share their rich inner world and give out what has taken them so long to assemble, the compulsive taker learns to give and to love in a new order.

Jesus as lover of wisdom

See Appendix 2: The Nine Enlightenments.

FIVEs identify with the Jesus who during his life longed for wisdom and went in search of it. We learn from the gospel narrative that when he was twelve years of age, Jesus' parents found him in the temple 'among the teachers'. Through his longing for knowledge and truth Jesus uncovered a route of wisdom which he wanted to share.

In common with FIVEs, Jesus had the ability to detach himself. The gospel records how he spent time alone, in prayer and in reflection, and then went on to convey his insights to his followers.

Jesus exercised discernment. He urged his disciples to discover truth through what he called 'the signs of the times'. Rubbing shoulders with people of all kinds, Jesus taught a rounded wisdom which included the ability to detect pretension, foolishness and bogus attitudes. Having pinpointed the shortcomings of the religious practice in his day, he moved swiftly to bring about enlightenment and renewal. He wanted to present with clarity what he regarded as paramount in God's eyes, as well as helping people to see through what was unimportant. He constantly challenged his adversaries to come to know the truth.

Because he spoke out of his own experience and conviction, those who heard Jesus found a freshness in his teaching. Jesus recognised that life itself was the best teacher. Matthew affirms: 'And when Jesus finished these sayings, the crowds were astonished at his teachings, for he taught them as one who had authority, and not as the scribes.'

Jesus invented original ways for presenting the truth he promulgated. He had the gift of the FIVE for precision. Some of his most important teachings he rolled together in telling phrases: 'Do not judge and you will not be judged'; 'My yoke is sweet and my burden light'; 'Do not be afraid'.

As a man of wisdom, Jesus taught his disciples how to let God speak directly to their hearts. Although he would often remove himself from the crowds, Jesus avoided the trap of the FIVE –

aloofness. Sometimes at great cost, he insisted on sharing his wisdom directly with others.

He opened his public ministry by living with a group of close friends and then systematically taught them his message of universal love and the wisdom of the Kingdom. He knew that wisdom demands contact with the process of events. It was always his intention that 'the word' would not remain in the realm of idea or philosophical opinion. It was to become flesh, relevant and world-changing. In the streets and the synagogues Jesus taught through stories and parables. He was a thinker who cared. Avoiding the cynicism of the FIVE, he encouraged his audience to extract the truth from him through their questioning. He appealed directly to their imagination. He wanted to impart what really mattered to them.

Jesus knew that to live wisely means to be present to each person and happening, able to detect God's love and truth through the gift of the moment. The wise person is not one who collects knowledge, but one who discovers truth.

Entering the Kingdom of God is like finding a new world within the present one. The Kingdom is of the present moment. But to discover it you need to become involved, not stand on the edge observing.

The gospel encounter with Jesus helps FIVEs to guard against:

- remaining on the edge of things, retaining wisdom for themselves and being introspective and uninvolved. Jesus said: 'If you love me, feed my lambs.'
- questioning everything, being miserly and too critical.
- engaging in endless projects that attempt to fill a deep inner emptiness but contribute little. The invitation is to surrender to the mystery of God.
- neglecting people's deepest feelings. God's work can suffer from too much objectivity.
- a failure to put themselves at the service of others and to ask for what they need.

Jesus shows FIVEs how to rejoice in:

- their ability to be objective and to take up new ideas. They have a gift of discernment.
- a capacity to move people to new ways of thinking.
- a love of learning and an appreciation of wisdom.
- their willingness to be patient and sympathetic listeners.
- a skill for objectivity and organisation.

Spur: To progress from a studied non-involvement at the periphery of life to a passionate engagement and sharing of the truth.

Way of prayer for The Observer

See Appendix 3: Prayer and the Enneagram.

FIVEs need to take seriously the Incarnation – the God who became man – and Christ's passion for the human condition, the Christ who became involved, who roughed it, who was rejected and crucified.

FIVEs must eventually quit the library of their lives and share their energies and insights with the world outside. This struggle will also mean they risk making mistakes.

The characteristic route of the FIVE personality is from the outside in. The spiritual journey will take the opposite direction – from the inside to the external. To discover balance and harmony, FIVEs have to move out of themselves. Their style of prayer will also take them in this direction. They have to let go of their mind perceptions, allowing heart and body to join the quest. Initially, in prayer, they will have to contest the swift tide of their thoughts and open up their heart centre.

In the formal prayer setting, it is helpful for them to concentrate on a symbol – a lighted candle, a crucifix, an icon or a mandala. This makes use of their natural preference for the visual, as well as instigating and keeping focus. A mantra will also discipline the mind and give structure to the meditation. Attention to posture will have the same impact. Praying with their eyes open, for example, serves to remind FIVEs of their need for external interaction. Encounter with their emotional lives will help them to move out of their carefully protected inner world.

Working against their natural compulsion, the FIVE personality benefits from a prayer style that touches their emotions. Because they are normally guarded in their expression of affection, methods that encourage warmth and spontaneity, such as dialogue, the use of a journal or rhythmic movement, will intensify their personal encounter in prayer. These styles will support them as they move into relationship. Required in this way to restrain their natural desire to attend to the many alternative voices competing for their attention, FIVEs will progress as they relax to the object of their meditation and project on to it something of their intense desire for God.

Particulary useful for the FIVE may be the adoption of the Jesus Prayer, with the double discipline of the mantra and following the breath. This can gradually create the conditions for an expressive engagement, surrender, single-mindedness and inner stillness.

The FIVE route to well-being

Unhealthy characteristics: reclusive, paranoid, obsessed
Average characteristics: analytical, abstract, eccentric
Redeemed characteristics: wise, visionary, innovative
Values: knowledge, security, objectivity
Time tendency: present
Strongest sense: sight
Emotion least controlled: fear
Domination: authority
Masks: withdrawal, confidence
Problems: uncertainty, fear

The FIVE surrenders

- I no longer demand to know more before I do anything.
- I let go of my inclination to avoid life by escaping into my mind.
- I abandon the agitation and restlessness of my mind.

The FIVE affirmations

- I affirm the value of my sense of humour.
- I say 'yes' to the struggles in my life, realising they are meaningful and rewarding.
- I now affirm that I can find peace in being compassionate towards others.

Pilgrim path for the FIVE personality

The Observer's route of intellect

FIVEs opt for the way of knowledge and of thinking. As we have seen, they trust the mind, stack up the facts and go in search of wisdom. The danger in this enterprise comes when it cuts them off from real living. As they continue to gather and hoard, they can withdraw and become stuck in the realm of the technical, the scientific or the metaphysical, running the risk of inhabiting a world of their own making. FIVEs can become enmeshed in

They need to join more openly with others.

a theoretical avoidance which may degenerate into isolation and a total insensitivity to the requirements of others.

The pilgrim path of the FIVE moves them towards the specific. Content for a while at least with not knowing the answers, they are eventually required to find the motivation to relate, become involved and engaged in individual, concrete encounters. As they do this, they will begin to feel at one with genuine needs and will attempt to grapple with them.

FIVEs must eventually stop thinking, trust their environment and the people in it, and become passionately immersed. Suppression of affection and avoidance of life must give way to doing and feeling. Keeping an open mind, using their curiosity and ability to sustain concentration, and prepared to ask penetrating questions, they seek to establish related patterns and true meanings.

Redeemed, the FIVE personality can exercise their objectivity and research skills to produce valuable and original ideas. As they put themselves and their ideas on the line, they can see with clarity and lead with confidence. At this point, accepting that the more they do the more they will learn, and rooting themselves in communal experience, they will fine-tune their commitment to help and enlighten others. They experience that this engagement begins to solve the problem of their own avarice. Scarcity has been the basic fear but Kingdom economics now underlines the reality that sharing and community actually create abundance. You either hoard or you share, and when you share you discover that even energy is plentiful.

FIVEs can enrich society as they follow the route of learning and journey towards the truth, especially the highest truths. They can innovate and enthuse, opening up fresh and perhaps even revolutionary territories of knowledge.

God image

FIVEs are comfortable with the God who has existed from all time. He is the Logos, the Word – the explanation of all things. This is a detached God who allows us to remain detached. The Christian God, of course, completes the paradox. Christ becomes man and participates in divine redemption. This is the God of involvement and commitment. The Incarnation highlights in stark form the route the FIVE personality must embrace.

When you meet a FIVE

- At times you will have the feeling that they want to retreat: don't take it personally. They have great need of their own space.
- If possible, give them a warning if you want to chat things through.
- You demonstrate your trust in them when you leave them to get on with the job. They don't hanker after approval.
- If you are asking for something, try not to put it in the shape of a demand.
- They are alive to silent signals and are apt to cut out if there is a lack of interest.
- State your own feelings but don't expect them to be able to express their feelings readily.
- Silence from them is not a sign of disapproval. It's often just their way of being.

The Supporter

10

FACE SIX

The Supporter

Loyalist, Guardian, Comrade, Team Player, Traditionalist, Devil's Advocate, Questioner, Friend-at-Court, Stalwart and Defender

Were the diver to think of the jaws of the shark he would never lay hands on the precious pearl.

Sa'di

My way: Supporting
My statement: 'I am loyal.'
My centre: Head
My passion: Doubt and anxiety
My compulsion: Security
My fear: Fear
My avoidance: Originality
My method: Authority and danger
My need: Faith
My virtue: Courage

Gift

The gift of the SIX personality motivates them to be loyal and hard-working. They are trustworthy and offer generous support particularly to those who have been neglected or unfairly treated. Productive and imaginative, they are prepared to work consistently without public recognition. They have a capacity for great self-sacrifice, particularly when real danger threatens. They are reliable and faithful to family, friends and the organisation.

SIXes as children have an acute sense of danger and they grow up experiencing much fear. They are naturally cautious and can be highly suspicious of new situations. They may have poor self-esteem and this can inhibit their progress. They sometimes try to avoid danger by keeping the rules and being generally conformist. They are naturally very hard-working.

SIXes are often plagued by doubt and fear about themselves and other people. Their caution leads them to procrastinate when it comes to decision-making. They see the negative aspects in any new challenge. But they are loyal to their friends and to any group they join. They are happier carrying out instructions and obeying the rules rather than taking the initiative themselves. They make good company people.

When they do break the rules, SIXes may have considerable difficulty in acknowledging this because of the shame they experience. They are much more likely to see the fault in others than in themselves.

SIXes like to know the precise pecking order. They sometimes have an undue regard for authority. They can resort to aggressive behaviour to counter any action they regard as a threat. They don't enjoy having their own opinions challenged. The wary SIX-type personality decides to do combat with what they fear and forcefully – but still fearfully – attempt to bring what they view as the enemy under control.

Likely to view most challenges as threats, SIXes usually avoid taking risks. They fear change and the unknown and can become anxious and aggressive. They can also be legalistic in their attitudes. Rules can play a big part in their lives and they may attempt to inflict these on others. They tend to be natural pessimists.

Because of their basic insecurity, they are also apt to be serious, secretive and mistrustful. They often have difficulty enjoying free time. They are mistrustful of their instincts and usually experience life as making great demands on them.

Whenever they perform well, they find difficulty in acknowledging their own contribution. They readily identify with the oppressed and are willing to champion their cause.

SIXes will be inclined to say 'yes' to most of the following statements:

- I work hard, I am reliable and like to get things done.
- I seem to be constantly working against or challenging my fears.
- I enjoy working alongside people I respect.
- I like to have limits in which to work.
- I seem to sense danger or threat more than other people do.
- I like to feel secure in my relationships.
- I am often blocked by doubt. Decision-making can be difficult.
- Loyalty to a group is very important to me.
- I trust my ability to be logical more than I trust my feelings.
- I can be anxious much of the time and don't like being blamed.

'I am loyal.'

Challenges confronting The Supporter

SIXes opt for thinking, and more specifically for worrying, as a substitute for action. The basic sin, which we have been calling the capital blindness, of the SIX is fear. The constant gospel admonition of Jesus, 'fear not', addresses this instinctive anxiety experienced in the SIX personality.

Fear is sometimes cloaked with the virtue of obedience. But false obedience is nothing more than the rotten fruit of fear, a cover for anxiety and an avoidance of courage.

It is essential for SIXes to name their fear for what it is – fear. They have to break with the inclination to call it faith, loyalty or even 'real faith'. Fear is a sin against faith in the widest sense and it can become a life stance. SIXes are initially challenged to come to terms with some counter-measures to their anxiety and fear by giving more scope to risk and allowing for the enjoyment of freedom and humour.

SIXes are suspicious of other people's motives. They have two ways of trying to soothe their own insecurity: by seeking a trustworthy protector and guide or by going against authority and adopting the role of the devil's advocate. They are caught up between the need to find a leader or credit-worthy organisation and deep mistrust of authoritarian structures.

Fearful of acting in their own right, SIXes will often dither when it comes to taking the plunge. Doubt may shape their habit, leading to serious procrastination.

Fundamentalists of every hue seek to discover an infallible source of uprightness. This search for correctness can cloak their attempts to counter their insecurity. Awareness of these forms of behaviour is the first step in reducing the influence of this outlook.

SIXes long for assurance and orderliness and can therefore be bedazzled by hierarchy, bureaucracy and assertive authorities. In nearly every situation SIXes want to know where they stand. They will often acknowledge they are more content when the chain of command is clear-cut. SIXes can simultaneously overestimate and mistrust authority. Because they feel vulnerable themselves, they are sometimes prepared to accept with blind obedience.

Most SIXes are particular about keeping to the letter of the law.

They also like to insist that others don't breach the law. They find the law and law-keeping – and at times even law-breaking – a source of fascination. They develop a sixth sense for suspicious circumstances.

Because they harbour a natural mistrust, SIXES readily anticipate the worst. This adds to fear and anxiety which they are very capable of projecting on to those around them. These negative scenarios can become what feels and looks like open hostility, even hatred.

SIXes often question their own capabilities. Harbouring a basic mistrust about themselves, they can easily fall into the trap of looking for and discovering these same traits in others. SIXes continually confirm their own worst fears. They will readily find scapegoats. They can conjure up a vision of how everything can go wrong. SIXes will constantly scan the horizon for threatening signs and they will watch closely to work out what is going on in people's minds.

But the basic challenge confronting the SIX is to claim their own inner authority. True self-reliance is based on this awareness and reduces dependence on external authorities. To overcome their fears they have to learn to trust. This is what the SIX personality wants most of all from life – to be free from fear. The danger is that they scale down their search and settle for security.

Hooks of the SIX

- Drawing a blank when it comes to success and pleasure.
- Endless doubt and scepticism.
- Loyalty and duty to the cause.

Route of integration for The Supporter

See Appendix 1: The Conversion Enterprise.

SIXes often have difficulty appreciating the value of their own giftedness: loyalty, willingness to sacrifice for the cause and a readiness to commit themselves in practical service.

Surprisingly, the particular grace of the SIX is courage. Above all other types in the Enneagram, and despite the fact that they have to battle so much with fear, they can grow to become the most courageous of people.

Unredeemed SIXes are lacking in self-confidence. Life invites them to discover faith in the sense of a willingness to journey into mystery. They have to open to their own giftedness. God trusts in us and looks for a response in kind. Precisely because God has confidence in us, we can develop a healthy self-confidence. In turn this can be used to support and lead others in significant communal enterprises which rely on self-sacrifice.

SIXes have to learn to trust themselves in this sense. Waiting for certitude they may never act at all. They have to discover from their own experience what is best for them. This route often starts by naming their fears. The SIX has to wrestle to be free from external direction and referring everything back to 'authorities'. It is essential for them to take responsibility for their own lives, decisions and feelings.

They are often blocked by doubt.

SIXes must seek personal trust in themselves and in God. The point is to develop an intimate, heart-based relationship to a personal God. It is fear which prevents them from risking this relationship.

SIXes find it helpful – but they may have to overcome their fears to do it – to join a community in which people open themselves and share their real fears and feelings. They need to develop the courage to communicate spontaneously. They may also find it helpful to test out their fears with their friends in order to detect and let go of the inconsequential – and SIXes are subject to many such fears. They are often tempted to take themseves too seriously. A more effective strategy is to keep recalling their successes and to use these as springboards to further progress.

It is essential for SIXes to encounter a God who doesn't punish or threaten them and allows them to make mistakes – their own mistakes. Ultimately they discover that trust and faith itself is life-giving.

To achieve integration within the Enneagram model, SIXes need to take on the positive aspects of the NINE. This will help them to:

- drop their suspicions and move towards trust. They will begin to allow others to know and love them and in this process they will find themselves accepted.
- discover their own inner calm and peace. Their doubts and fears will begin to lessen and they will begin at last to experience their own centre as durable and worthy of trust.
- avoid giving undue weight to the opinions of others. They will start to take responsibility for their own actions and question authority figures. They will stop demanding impossible standards of themselves.
- avoid outlandish responses. When under pressure they keep their fears under strict control.
- become more realistic about their own feelings and more direct in the expression of these feelings.

The Supporter: Symbols and Invitation

The symbols are used here as a description of some of the energies displayed by the SIX personality, the Supporter.

Animal: Wolf
The wolf invests for its safety in its sight. For security it depends on the strength of the pack. Here there is order, rank and authority. The wolf knows that the lone wolf is a myth. Security lies with the pack. The instinct of the wolf is for survival and its duty is to be loyal to the pack leader. The wolf shows an instinct for authority and for parenting. Within the pack there is also a sense of formation and education. Obedience and order have to be imbued. The wolf's disciplined life follows a predictable schedule. The aggressive wolf puppy needs correction. If he fails to respond, the parent wolf will take him out and break his neck. A system of law is essential. Everyone in the outside world is regarded with suspicion. External opposition is best destroyed. SIXes, like the wolf, tend to be dutiful and dependable, at times conscientious to a fault.

Country: Germany
The stereotypical image of regimented Germany matches this masculine energy – artificial self-assurance which covers for uncertainty. This repression of fear can be traced in German history. There is a determination to believe that the leader is trustworthy. Opposition to lawful authority is seen as malicious.

Colour: The symbolic colour of the SIX is beige. On its own it doesn't draw the eye, but it is still expressive. Like beige, SIXes are adaptable in any environment. Beige/brown is the combination of red and green but the result does not belong to the classic colour spectrum. It conveys closeness to the earth and security.

Beliefs
- Life is dangerous so be prepared.
- Keep your distance. Being vulnerable leads to pain.
- I have to do my duty.

Queries

- Is there any danger in this?
- What is going to hit me next?

Childhood message: Nothing seems to be reliable. There were experiences of humiliation. Parents may have been perceived as unpredictable and therefore adequate protection became very difficult. Self-defence was problematic. Authority figures were distant and could even be violent.

Invitation: Towards trust

SIXes are invited to embrace faith, to move into what at first sight can only be described as darkness. They have to travel into mystery. This calls them into a relationship of trust – a trust of self, of neighbour, and ultimately of God.

SIXes are challenged to take responsibility for their lives, to make their own decisions. They need to identify and name their fears in order to break the trap of trepidation.

Growth begins when they give themselves some credit for their successes. Humour has a part to play in driving out their fears and freeing them for further action. They see through their own anxious stance, move through their hesitancy and refuse to take themselves too seriously.

SIXes need to journey towards a love that is positive and secure, resting on the conviction of faith. They find trust in a love they eventually recognise as never absent. It is faithful, warm and committed.

They come to discover that God has supreme belief and trust in us and we in turn are invited to make this mutual. Discovering God's confidence brings us directly to self-confidence. Perfect love – the Holy Spirit within – casts out fear.

Ultimately SIXes are invited to move through fear into the high virtue of courage. Discovering they cannot be separated from God's love, they unearth the courage within to take bold initiatives on behalf of others, summoning those around them to do the same.

Jesus as the loyal supporter

See Appendix 2: The Nine Enlightenments.

As recorded in the gospel narrative, Jesus demonstrates the strengths of the personality types of the Enneagram system while, at the same time, remaining free from the obsessional traits within each type. The gospel indicates, for example, how Jesus was prepared to sacrifice himself completely for the cause as he lived out the role of faithful servant of God.

The aim of the SIX personality in the Enneagram system will be to relate to Jesus as a model of loyalty, a loyalty highlighted in the gospel by the specific dedication of Jesus to his own Jewish people, the people of God.

Jesus came to see his task as a fulfilment of the scriptures, while fully accepting the burdens this inevitably imposed. He had come 'not to be served, but to serve'. Jesus was especially loyal to those close to him. He both lived this fidelity and taught it: 'A man can have no greater love than to lay down his life for his friends. You are my friends. . . .'

SIXes can see their own virtue of being the faithful servant mirrored in many of the gospel stories. We see, for example, how Jesus met his obligation to his mother when, during his passion, he asked his favourite disciple, John, to take care of her.

It is also clear that Jesus had little use for worldly power structures. He told his disciples: 'Whoever would be great among you must be your servant, and whoever would be first among you must be your slave.' He rejected the rules when they trapped people instead of serving them. SIXes may be readily trapped by fear and uncertainty, but Jesus repeatedly called on people to overcome their fears and to trust in God: 'Do not be afraid, only believe.'

SIXes, as we have seen, can be tempted to take their loyalty too far and slip into legalism. There is a lesson here for Christ's followers. There is always a danger that the observance of rules can become an end in itself rather than a means. Morality and religion can be focused too readily on adherence to the maxims. This style of religion can feed the insecurity of the SIX. By keeping to rules they can claim to remain under God's observance. But Jesus wanted his followers to be free: 'I have come that you may have life and have it more abundantly.' The measure of this fullness was not to be the rule book.

Along with adherance to written laws, SIXes may attempt to achieve security by carrying out the orders of someone in authority. In situations of uncertainty, SIXes often look to an external authority for a solution. Obsession with the regulations and the rubrics can also lead to self-righteousness. But the Jesus story demonstrates that the spirit of the law is more important than the 'letter of the law'. A too strict observance can prevent the ripening of a deep relationship with God. Keeping the law then becomes the means of salvation rather than a trusting surrender to the grace of God.

Jesus always insisted that God was more than a lawgiver. He is Abba, loving parent. We recognise this when we imitate God by being compassionate, forgiving and just. Jesus gave a primacy to the love of God and love of neighbour. Religion is about salvation in terms of a right relationship with God, union with God – a submission of hope. The inner authority of Jesus stemmed from his trusting relationship with his heavenly Father.

The gospel encounter with Jesus will help SIXes to guard against:

- holding back because of uncertainty and doubt.
- being too cautious, distrustful, nervous and shy. Jesus wants his followers to walk into the light.
- a willingness to give up their independence for the sake of a greater love.
- putting too much emphasis on fidelity to rules.

Jesus shows SIXes how to rejoice in:

- their prudence and a willingness to take responsibility.
- an ability to have warm-hearted friendships marked by deep feelings and loyalty.
- their capacity to protect and be constant to those they love.
- a discovery within themselves of foresight and courage.
- their ability to be compassionate. The individual remains important for the SIX. They are called to exercise this intimate care and responsibility.

Spur: To move from fear and excessive caution to practical service and courageous support.

Way of prayer for The Supporter

See Appendix 3: Prayer and the Enneagram.

The Supporter, the SIX personality in the Enneagram system, is defensive by nature and moves towards protection. But progress in the spiritual journey calls them in the opposite direction, towards abandonment and surrender. Their integration, as with all the Enneagram types, depends on a willingness to become who they truly are. They have to allow their emotional and spiritual lives to be touched and healed, so they can accept themselves as worthy of deep love in their own right. They have to break through their own inner world of caution and fear.

When we pray we respond to the invitation to come close to God. Initially, SIXes instinctively avoid this style of letting go. They will make great efforts to curb the risk of spontaneity. Prayer helps them to contact their deepest feelings, to discover acceptance and trust, recognising their true worth in God's eyes. This experience of God's abiding and unconditional love is at the core of the interior life.

Opening to this ever-present and loving God, talking directly to him as they would to a trusted friend, SIXes will deepen their relationship. They may then be in a position to break through their set pattern and security addiction which could have the effect of preventing them from deeper engagement. They have to alight on a way of prayer that quests past fear and plunges into trust and intimacy.

A robust, conversational style of prayer can therefore be helpful to the SIX. Here they can let in their emotions. They can put their reality into words, reveal their fears and feelings, share their doubts, hopes and plans, and give full expression to their needs.

In the same way, contact with creation, an appreciation for nature which fosters thanksgiving, can kindle their desire for God. The gifts of creation help SIXes to move out from their heads and from themselves, allowing for spontaneous response and heartfelt expression.

As we have seen, SIXes may have to battle with what can become an endless tide of worries. They find freedom from the tyranny of their own ideas and fears in expressive and physical forms of prayer, which may employ music, movement and dance. SIXes can also adapt well to the flow of the Church's liturgical year.

These techniques, which may progress to include creative arts, liturgical dance or yoga postures, encourage personal responsibility and foster flexibility of mind and body as well as helping the SIX in awareness and self-acceptance. Self-trust can start here, leading on to deep self-abandonment. As they learn to value themselves and take further risks, they become aware of their own real and valuable inner treasures.

As we have seen, for the SIX, a personal awareness of the Spirit within transforms the source of their authority. This is the encounter which points them through their insecurity to ultimate trust.

The SIX route to well-being

Unhealthy characteristics: dependent, insecure, aggressive
Average characteristics: dutiful, ambivalent, indecisive
Redeemed characteristics: loyal, trusting, courageous
Values: security, conformity
Time tendency: future
Strongest sense: sight
Emotion least controlled: fear
Domination: authority
Mask: obedience
Problems: insecurity, abandonment

The SIX surrenders

- I no longer need to blame others for my own problems and mistakes.
- I let go of my fear of being abandoned and left alone.
- I give up my inclination to be negative and complaining.

The SIX affirmations

- I affirm I have faith in myself, my talents and my future.
- I say 'yes' to my ability to be calm and confident.
- I now affirm that I am secure and able to make the best of what comes my way.

Pilgrim path for the SIX personality

The Supporter's route of fidelity

The most essential quest for the SIX personality in the Enneagram system is to come to his or her own truth. SIXes may be tempted to postpone this arrival. Most of life can be over before they are set free to serve. In some measure this is of course true of all of us, but in a particular way, because they have such a crucial communal role to play, it is easier to see how this applies to SIXes. Society pays a heavy price whenever a SIX fails to integrate.

They need faith in themselves.

Healthy SIXes are able to commit themselves deeply. They also want others to respond to them. Having close ties with family and friends makes them feel they are not alone. The choices they make and the bonds they create often involve real identifications. They are highly regarded for their reliability. In intricate ways much depends on them.

When healthy, SIXes are playful and unpredictable. They want to be liked and they have childlike qualities. They can fight for you as they would for themselves. But only when their own inside work is advanced are they free enough to undertake for the rest of us what needs to be done. Loyalty to their own truth brings the SIX the necessary freedom to act.

They are loyal to the status quo. They are the pivotal point of the family; the hearth in the ancestral home. They have a corporate talent which, if withheld, puts the rest of us in trouble. There is a humility and a groundedness about them which must find expression within and on behalf of society. Without the necessary bonding all the superstructures are in danger of collapse.

In the end it is crucial that SIXes learn to affirm themselves and see through the bogus and the unworthy. They have to discover the true meaning of self-confidence and curb the wayward reactions to their own feelings. It is essential for them to become their own person. Only then are they capable of loving and of being loved. When at last they find faith in themselves, they are on the royal road to courage. Then they can stop protecting themselves, sift the truth and open to the goodness and value of a particular cause or humanity in general. Once integrated, emotionally stable and spiritually at home, they are able to commit themselves in a vital way to the welfare of society.

God image

SIXes readily relate to God as saviour. This is the God of the Psalms who is eternally trustworthy, the God who delivers his friends from their enemies. They relate to the God who promises security. So far so good. The danger is that this steadfastness prevents them from moving on. God is more than a rock. God may also want us to move into the desert, into the darkness of loss and suffering.

When you meet a SIX

- Encourage them to see the positive and to laugh at themselves. Remember, they struggle with doubt and find it hard to trust.
- Don't be surprised if they seem reluctant to accept your praise or compliments.
- Reassure them by the way you listen. Tell them that you love them.
- Realise that they are encouraged when you do what you say. They may even trust you – which is never easy for them.
- Don't be too harsh on their fears. Remember they have great commitment, even when they are full of doubt.

The Optimist

11

FACE SEVEN
The Optimist

Inspirer, Enthusiast, Connoisseur, Adventurer, Multi-Tasker, Planner, Player, Storyteller, Energiser, Life and Soul of the Party

Joy is the serious business of heaven.

C. S. Lewis

My way: Optimism
My statement: 'I am cheerful.'
My centre: Head
My passion: Gluttony
My compulsion: Idealism
My fear: Pain
My avoidance: Pain
My method: Planning for good times
My need: Balance
My virtue: Temperance

Gift

The gift of the SEVEN personality motivates them to bring imagination, cheerfulness and energy to the tasks of life. Extroverts, gregarious and innovative, they can reach out to people and engender enthusiasm. They enjoy bringing people and ideas together, particularly with a view to enhancing communal involvement. Talkative and often multi-talented, they view life as full of possibilities for further enjoyment.

As children SEVENs are likely to be full of charm and fun. They are cheerful and outgoing. They aim each day to maximise and radiate the joyful. This can hide the fact that deep down they are afraid.

In a bid to escape pain they switch their attention to the fun aspects of life. They are always in danger, as they move out towards others, of sacrificing quality for quantity. They avoid the frightening and the painful and they concentrate, often to the exclusion of almost everything else, on the lighthearted and the frothy. Expansive and entertaining, they put up the shutters against the more serious aspects of life.

SEVENs are convivial, optimistic and fun-loving. They are free spirits who seek out like-minded people. Prolific planners and constantly on the lookout to organise a full programme of activities, they will go to extraordinary lengths to avoid pain in all its aspects. They hope that endless, flexible planning will protect them against any burdensome tasks or duties that need to be tackled.

They like to keep their options open. In practice they tend to be late for most things. They procrastinate and avoid real commitments. They are excellent conversationalists and enjoy telling endless stories. They insist that life really belongs to the merrymakers and they can become compulsively jovial.

Because of their packed social agenda, and the speed with which they seek new environments, they will postpone dealing with deeper personal, social and spiritual issues. They find serious endeavours hard to sustain and seek escape through pleasure. In fact, SEVENs readily opt for over-indulgence and have problems with sobriety. They avoid confrontation by searching out more pleasant activities and can be caught up in addictive behaviour.

They have charm and endless plans in reserve, but they tend to impose these schemes without thinking how others are feeling. They take the view that by planning they can make everyone happy. They look for instant gratification and can become very aggressive when others try to advise restraint and self-control. By nature they are anti-authoritarian. They are the most optimistic of the Enneagram types.

SEVENs are likely to say 'yes' to most of the following statements:

- I like to keep the conversation light and cheerful.
- I like to savour the good things in life.
- I don't think it is wise to be sad for too long.
- I'm all for variety and endless choices.
- I like most of the people in my life.
- I like to think that other people see me as happy.
- I avoid boredom by keeping on the go.
- I'm too much of an optimist to dwell on life's problems.
- The sharing of deep emotions can make me feel uncomfortable.
- I can enjoy telling my boss the truth.

Challenges confronting The Optimist

SEVENs are the happy-go-lucky souls who look to bring joy to themselves and others in their circle. They are inclined to put off

'I am cheerful.'

facing up to any aspect of their life which may prove to be hurtful to themselves or to others.

A SEVEN will often rationalise in order to soften pain. In a failed relationship, for example, rational reasons for the failure will be clung to and the positive aspects of a new situation will be swiftly proposed. They also like to escape from their fears through the ready hatch of imagination.

The SEVEN is reluctant to experience pain. Sufferings, hardships and setbacks, irrespective of their formats, will usually be shifted rather than felt. Duties can loom as painful and the inclination to avoid these commitments by opting for the endlessly cheerful can be disconcerting, especially for those who are close to them. Optimism is at root highly virtuous, but the Enneagram inevitably warns the SEVEN personality against a buoyancy bordering on make-believe.

Breezy SEVENs tend to exaggerate their own image and can be readily cock-a-hoop to a fault. They can go cheerfully on for years without acknowledging the shadow side of life. They often have great difficulty dealing with emotional problems. Because they want everything to be sparkling, they dim out the other aspects of reality.

SEVENs have an excessive need for the pleasurable, for fun and for joy. They need to be plotting for the good times ahead. They will put enormous resources into this exercise. They have a talent for cheering up and enthusing other people and have an uncanny ability to attract their own type and create a fun-loving team. But when things move towards the deep or serious, the SEVEN will instinctively switch on his banter button or dive into his ample store of frivolous quips and anecdotes.

Occasionally, the clubbable SEVENs will come to recognise that their fun-loving front is just that, and that their grins cover a deep sadness that prevents them from dealing with their fears. But even then they will be tempted to keep misgivings at bay with fantasies of the likely successes awaiting them just over the horizon. They can long for someone to see through their charade and take their pain seriously. Often these signals are not taken up by others precisely because of the optimistic vibes which SEVENs naturally discharge. They usually have the added disadvantage of never looking afraid. Close associates are incredulous when they come to realise that their hospitable companion is really troubled deep down. All too readily the SEVEN may be forced to return to the familiar stance: 'Be happy.'

The capital blindness of the SEVEN is intemperance or gluttony. This is the nub of the challenge they face. It is not a gluttony restricted to food but extends to all the good things of life. More for the SEVEN is never enough.

They can exaggerate most things. More travelling, more sleep, more buying, more possessions, more fun and even more work. There is often little scope for restraint. Visions and plans feed their enthusiasms. They seek endless adventure. They have a particular gift for embellishing the amusing story and for squeezing from it the last drop of absurdity. Many SEVENs just talk too much. They are called to sober up in every sense.

They are inclined to devour science fiction and fantasy. They can be travel fanatics and Star Wars freaks. They believe that moving to some new place is bound to bring them more happiness.

The gift of the SEVEN is joy. But this should not be adopted to the total exclusion of the painful aspects of life. A false optimism should not be allowed to counter reality. They are challenged permanently to move towards sobriety. SEVENs have to learn the art of self-denial in order to come to the grace of sober joy. They have to slim down their search for options. This calls for serious surrender. What is most desired must be most abandoned.

Hooks of the SEVEN

- Talking, planning and dreaming.
- An endless stream of happenings. Keeping the options open.
- Using charm as a way of defence. Talking their way out of trouble.

Route of integration for The Optimist

See Appendix 1: The Conversion Enterprise.

SEVENs must come to grips with their intemperance. Their temptation is to place too little value on restraint. They have to take a hard look at the adage 'More is never enough'.

SEVENs need to discern wherever this gluttony is operative in their lives and then introduce the necessary disciplines. Here we sample the cutting edge of what we are calling conversion and growth. The inner way is not open to short cuts. There is always a price to pay.

The very idea of conversion for a SEVEN is likely to trigger the pain button. Their next response will be to escape. They have no relish for critical thinking. They will instinctively fall back on their very real charm or dredge up a joke that's doing the rounds – but only if it's funny enough.

SEVENs are called to co-operation with God and with life. As they begin to yield to this process they start to face up to reality and therefore to some pain, even desolation. They have to let

They fear pain in all its aspects.

their endless interests, friends and wanderings give way to deeper, quieter, more solitary moments. Priority choices are called for. Then they will begin to acknowledge their shadow, slow down and become accepting of that part of life that is without beauty and delight. At least occasionally, they need to let their endless fund of stories dip away.

As we have seen, the Enneagram labels sober joy as the gift of the redeemed SEVEN. The gift becomes compassionate and deep as it moves away from the addiction to pleasure. Consuming has to be replaced by savouring. They have to stop leaning into the future and curb their anticipation of the next fun event.

Gradually, as they become more reflective and responsible, they move towards a deeper self-acceptance and this will ultimately be the fruit of the realisation that as well as being accepted and cherished by their friends, they can also open themselves to God's transcendent love, the pre-eminent route of optimism. They can then begin to travel lighter and live in a world that is at once beautiful, pleasant and joyful but also painful. As they progress in their conversion, SEVENs look inwards and come to terms with their exaggerated fear of physical and psychological pain.

This is why a period of discipline, sickness or imposed restraint can move them towards insight, joy and the possibility of helping themselves and others confront their pain. The art of staying in one place begins to pay off. They come to know that real happiness is an inside job, a compassionate sharing, and not dependent on an endless search for gratification.

The gifts of the SEVEN, the blessing of good humour, a sense of adventure and the crucial grace of being able to see the ridiculous side of life, need to be set free for the community. Then the SEVEN finds real purpose and fulfilment.

The way of integration for the SEVEN is to move towards the best aspects of the FIVE. These will help them to:

- get to the heart of things instead of staying on the edges or being stuck in the superficial.
- face up to pain when necessary and resist the temptation always to avoid the serious.
- give as well as take. They need to curb their appetite for immediate gratification.

- discipline their impetuosity. They have to become selective about their enthusiasms. The restless urge for new things, new people, new places needs to be held in check.
- enter into their own space, solitude and silence.

The Optimist: Symbols and Invitation

Here we reflect on symbols appropriate for the SEVEN personality.

Animal: Otter
The otter is the clown of the animal kingdom. It loves to entertain and spends hours each day in open play. The otter is curiosity personified. It has keen sight and a voracious appetite. When they congregate – and otters enjoy community – they pose a significant threat to commercial fisheries. The otter has large eyes and loves to investigate its surroundings. As soon as it becomes bored it moves on to something new.

Country: Polynesia Islands
Hawaii captures the world of the otter. The Polynesian culture enjoys an abundance of food and play. The people are welcoming and friendly and the ocean waves plentiful and proximate. There is a Peter Pan sheen to the wearers of this skin – a reluctance to grow up. They are natural entertainers with a happy disposition and a ready smile. They see life as full of endless possibilities.

Colour: The symbolic colour of the SEVEN is green – the colour of new life. Green symbolises fresh hope and well-being. Green also stands, in colloquial language, for naive and childish behaviour. Green can remind SEVENs that their maturing process will demand more than *joie de vivre* and the lush pastures of a welcome springtime.

Beliefs
- Life is a party.
- Nothing is that serious.
- Keep your options open.

Queries

- What's in this for me?
- Am I as good as I think I am?
- Isn't more always better?

Childhood message: Their experience led SEVENs to believe that it is good to escape into fantasy, that it helps to relieve the pain. The past is remembered as beautiful, childhood as a dream. Pain, they feel, is best forgotten. 'Let's talk about the wonderful times. We pumped everything up and it was great.'

Invitation: Towards true happiness

SEVENs can reach the stage where they plan their good times so well, they forget how to be spontaneous. Then they are no longer at ease with their gift for celebration. They can become especially tense in their determination to avoid pain. Fear feeds their mood swings and can make them retreat from reality.

The gift of the redeemed SEVEN is a balanced, sober joy. To achieve this SEVENs have to find their way to a deep self-acceptance. Then they can live realistically with the beautiful or the messy. At this point the dreams of the past and the visions of the future lose their hold.

A selected discipline may become a source of joy. They must find a way to digest their pain, to explore their darkness. They have to slow down their lives to the point where they can see themselves as they truly are – co-creators.

SEVENs are invited to co-operate with God. In order to achieve this they have to make themselves available at a deeper level. Then at last they can confront the reality of a world not of their own making and mixed with joy and pain.

New life follows from dying to oneself. Joy follows from pain endured with patience. To be involved in God's creative process has the effect of increasing our capacity for acceptance of disappointments and suffering. In this way SEVENs abandon themselves to God. This is their holy work. A true spirituality will take them through anxiety and death to resurrection.

Jesus as the enthusiast

See Appendix 2: The Nine Enlightenments.

Jesus clearly enjoyed having a good time with his friends. SEVENs will appreciate this postive aspect of Jesus' personality. His enemies accused him of enjoying wine and avoiding the frugal life adopted by the prophet John the Baptist. Jesus' response was to see himself in the role of the bridegroom, saying that being with him was like being a guest at a wedding party. This was no moment for sadness. Jesus here was pointing to the celebratory nature of his mission and, again, SEVENs will readily accord with the freedom to be joyful which Jesus emphasised.

In the same way, the gospel story highlights the wedding party at Cana as a sign of the abundance of the Kingdom of God made present in the person and actions of Jesus. At Mary's request, Jesus presents the party with a surfeit of the best wine. Jesus went on to compare heaven with an everlasting wedding celebration. He told people God wanted them to rejoice because they have every cause to do so. Jesus' central message, the coming of the Reign of God, is good news and he proclaims it at every opportunity. He declares it to be a Kingdom already made available. This Kingdom 'at hand' consists of a communal enjoyment of the gifts of God to all believers. To participate in the Kingdom it is necessary to know how to enjoy life.

The optimistic SEVENs can readily relate to Jesus as a person whose heart longs for the good things as we wait for the totality of the promises of God. Jesus enjoyed being invited to dinner and it seemed to make little difference where the invitations came from – tax collectors, lepers, Pharisees or close friends and supporters.

Again, in the eucharist, Jesus chose a banquet of food and drink – a way of enjoyment rather than a route of self-denial – as a permanent symbol for Christians to use down the ages in thanksgiving to God for the gift of salvation.

But, as we have seen, the hook of the fun-loving SEVENs is revealed in the problems they have with pain in all its forms. Their temptation is to avoid what proves costly, to procrastinate and over-indulge in the pleasurable.

As they move towards maturity, SEVENs come to appreciate that it is unrealistic to expect everything to be fun. Jesus demonstrated that evil often needs to be overcome by acceptance which may include setbacks and much suffering. There is purpose in this anguish. Troubles produce patient endurance and hopeful expectation. Commitment becomes a communal virtue which releases its own energy in the contest for justice.

The gospel encounter with Jesus will help SEVENs to guard against:

- withdrawal under pain and pressure. Jesus accepts painful human reality, even to death on the cross.
- excessive day-dreaming. They over-idealise good situations and may live in the future to avoid the pain of the present.
- being insensitive to the way in which they impose their plans on others.
- having abstract visions that are not put into practice.
- being too demanding. They keep looking for immediate response.
- their reluctance to probe at a deeper level.

Jesus shows SEVENs how to rejoice in:

- their readiness to be cheerful and to celebrate life.
- their ability to see giftedness in everything and to delight in life and in nature.
- their sensitivity to others. Jesus is sensitive to the unspoken need for forgiveness in the paralytic.
- their ability to communicate enthusiasm and the great gift of humour.
- their ability to identify possibilities. They have an inner vision of how things can work.

Spur: To change from superficial extrovert and compulsive planner to trustworthy source of balanced joy.

Way of prayer for The Optimist

See Appendix 3: Prayer and the Enneagram.

Constantly planning to bring about a brighter tomorrow, and jostling to reduce the boredom and pain of the moment, SEVENs run the risk of becoming over-involved. But even at an ordinary level, their spiritual journey can help them to bring in some necessary restraint and depth. The direction of the journey for the SEVEN is from the inside out. They have to engage with life outside of themselves.

On the other hand, some forms of charismatic prayer with their tendency towards large groupings, expressive declaration and a robust hymnology, have been labelled SEVEN in style. There is a determination to be happy, to court the excessive, and critics, with some justification, point to a reluctance to face the painful and the negative in life, an unwillingness to embrace the Cross.

In reality all of life is intended to be prayer, neither the joy nor the pain is excluded, and SEVENs are gradually called to open up to this. Kingdom reality nearly always dawns slowly. To recover their point of balance, SEVENs in prayer have to learn to slow down, come into the moment, clip back on their own hidden agenda and confront reality.

In set meditation this means creating the conditions for some degree of stillness and receptivity and focusing attention. SEVENs may have to acknowledge their own restlessness at this stage and persist in their quest for depth.

A relaxed posture can be an important beginning, projecting on to the symbol (whether crucifix, statue, icon, picture or mandala) their desire for God. Use of the Jesus prayer, concentrating initially perhaps on the meaning of the words, focusing on breathing and coming into the moment, will nurture a relaxed concentration and this may lead on, for example, to the prayer of gratitude.

In the same way, to pray with their eyes open can allow scope for passive acceptance, some inner stillness. SEVENs have to simplify their multiple choices. This helps them towards that single-mindedness and state of unity in prayer where they are seeking nothing else but God. It is good to remind ourselves when considering prayer techniques that unless the changes triggered are genuine, and the transformation real, we could be just wasting our time.

Initially SEVENs must be willing to let go of the merry-go-round of their own making. To be single-pointed and open to the presence of God, they have to be aware of their need to discipline the call of the many alternative voices that clamour so persistently for their attention.

SEVENs often have a natural relish for the beautiful and the harmonious. To fly a kite, to climb a high mountain, to sit by a lake and feel part of the immensity of nature, is to open to the enjoyment of life's banquet.

Allowing for their sensate nature through touch, taste and smell, immersing themselves in creation rather than just observing it, SEVENs can respond wholeheartedly and let God do the initiating in their lives. This direct use of the senses can help the SEVEN to stay with the self, to curb a readiness to run away, and to accept that true joy lies within. In the same way, they can confront the paradoxical in their lives, the happiness and the sadnesses, and learn to live contentedly with this bitter-sweet result.

The SEVEN route to well-being

Unhealthy characteristics: excessive, impulsive, escapist
Average characteristics: hyperactive, superficial, unrealistic
Redeemed characteristics: appreciative, enthusiastic, versatile
Values: harmony, security, joy
Time tendency: future
Strongest sense: sight
Emotion least controlled: fear
Domination: authority
Masks: community, plans, fantasy
Problems: insecurity, freedom

The SEVEN surrenders

- I no longer burn myself out by trying to meet all my desires.

- I let go of the feeling that I always need more.
- I abandon my belief that external things will make me happy.

The SEVEN affirmations

- I affirm that I can say no to myself without feeling deprived.
- I say 'yes' to the spiritual dimension.
- I now affirm that I can find satisfaction in ordinary things.

Pilgrim path for the SEVEN personality

The Optimist's route of festivity

SEVENs find themselves on the path of celebration. This is the way of happiness. It is a vital route which all of us resonate with and will, in part at least, always need. This is another wondrous vocational way that needs to be shared as well as enjoyed.

The route of festivity, joy and delight led by the SEVEN also calls for discipline. The excesses in the search for the good time

They need to find the right balance in their lives.

have to be curbed. Festivity needs to be harnessed and refined. On this magnetic path the lure of instant and excessive gratification remains a threat.

SEVENs, as we have seen, need to open to the dark and the painful in their lives. The healthy SEVEN learns to celebrate life for what it is. Their appreciation sharpened, they begin to sense that they possess enough to make them happy. They acquire the ability and the enthusiasm to respond to the joy of each and every occasion. This vitality is infectious and all of us need to draw energy from this route.

SEVENs need to trust their optimism. They have to overcome their fear of being deprived. They enjoy a physical elixir and an enthusiasm which includes a capacity to be endlessly recharged. Again, we all stand in need of a slice of their humour, their ability to diffuse the burdensome and their know-how for turning the ordinary into a blessing. SEVENs have the gift of keeping their lives green – a ready smile, a freshness of thought and enterprise, a willingness to acknowledge the giftedness of life.

Integrated SEVENs will allow themselves to move on from consumer to contemplator and their sense of gratitude will blossom into feelings of awe and wonder for creation. They will bring the full force of their talents and imagination to their own experiences. Eventually they touch the holy and celebrate it.

When life has been deeply experienced, the inner route of the SEVEN can itself become a dynamic reality. SEVENs can lead others to this banquet, bringing experiences rich and entirely original to the world.

God image

SEVENs can relate to the God of delight. They can readily empathise with the God of all creation, the cause of eternal beauty. Easter's paschal mystery includes death and resurrection, and the SEVEN has to struggle to take in the entirety of this mystery. The Risen Christ brings joy – but at a price. The true Christ felt the heat of the day. He suffered death on the Cross.

When you meet a SEVEN

- You can keep them to the task in hand by asking questions, including questions about how they feel.
- They like you to join in their banter. Try to enjoy their stories and their dreams. You may have heard it before, but they will probably tell it differently anyway.
- Watch your criticism – they may take it personally. Try not to give them instructions.
- Be open to their plans. Don't take the whole thing too seriously. Only some of the adventures will actually happen.

The Leader

12

FACE EIGHT

The Leader

Fighter-boss, Protector, Contender, Provider, Maverick, Militant, Entrepreneur, Rebel, Challenger and Commander

If we are passionate, meaning compassionate, there is hope.

Elie Wiesel

My way: Leadership
My statement: 'I am strong.'
My centre: Gut
My passion: Lust
My compulsion: To be in charge
My fear: Weakness
My avoidance: Subordination
My method: Power
My need: Tenderness
My virtue: Simplicity

Gift

The gift of the EIGHT personality motives them to take charge of the enterprises they are involved in. They are natural leaders. They enjoy power and control and are apt to work hard and play hard. They value truth, fairness and integrity. They can inspire others and are particularly generous to their friends. They can be protective and empowering and can use their authority to combat injustice. They are self-assertive, courageous and enjoy fresh challenges.

As children EIGHTs rapidly come to the conclusion that they can deny their fear and vulnerability and challenge for leadership by exerting their power. They decide that the more aggressive they are, the more likely it is they can have their own way.

EIGHTs believe that other people also enjoy standing up for themselves and they are on the lookout for fights. They are quick to exploit any weakness on the horizon. They have scant regard for the feelings of others and can at times be quite cruel. They are very reluctant to apologise.

EIGHTs are often openly aggressive and love to challenge and dominate others. By throwing tantrums and through outbursts of anger they attempt to dominate those around them. They regard life as a battle. They are naturally competitive and like to seek out the weakest point in the opposition. They enjoy using aggressive and coarse language.

They prefer to have things out in the open and they will let you know when they are displeased. They do not like underhanded methods and they will seek to expose these in others.

EIGHTs despise weakness and maintain respect only for those who are prepared to fight their corner. They like to provoke people in order to find out what makes them tick. They seek conflict, and sometimes, when they don't find it, they create it. They can be frank to the point of rudeness. They like to project an image of hardness.

EIGHTs have a lust for life. They are prepared to take risks and to defend the under-dog, especially if they are the victims of injustice. They enjoy struggles, confrontation and the display of power. They can be fiercely courageous in defending what they regard as right. They are good people to have on your side. When caught up in a project, they can work with great commitment.

EIGHT personalities like to know where they stand. They love a contest and won't count the cost. They look for the opportunity to take risks and have enormous endurance of pain. They enjoy shocking other people. They can be very protective of their friends but their relationships may be based on submission.

EIGHTs will say 'yes' to most of the following statements:

- I am prepared to stand up and fight for what I want.
- I can be moved by the hurts and sufferings of others.

- I am not afraid to confront other people.
- I get bored easily and like to keep moving.
- I am reluctant to acknowledge weakness in myself.
- I have a sense of where the power lies in a group.
- I can be ruthless and driven by revenge.
- I am a bit of a rebel and am often reluctant to conform.
- People respect power. Money goes hand in hand with power.
- I can make things happen and get projects finished.

Challenges confronting The Leader

EIGHTs are passionate lovers of life. They like to appoint themselves as avengers. They also enjoy seeing themselves as protectors. They readily take up the role of justice-maker and defender of the weak. They are constantly searching for someone to defend or to take in hand and punish. Their method is the exacting of justice through retaliation. They will insist that the 'bad' person has to be

'I am strong.'

punished, even if the 'bad' person happens to be themselves. EIGHTs have little respect for the weakest.

The style of the EIGHT is to take control. They like to put those around them to the test. In positions of authority – to which they naturally gravitate – they will be on the lookout for a complete takeover. They don't favour equal alliances.

It is vital to recognise the little child in the EIGHT who is vulnerable and trusting. EIGHTs themselves have to learn to understand that this vulnerability also exists outside of themselves and that they can defend and cherish it on behalf of others.

EIGHTs are challenged to acknowledge their personal vulnerability, their own child within, and to come to terms with this weakness. They will normally go to great pains to avoid this. They need to be honest and sincere and willing to accept the tender side of their nature.

EIGHTs are usually strong, adventurous and combative. They opt to defend themselves by denial. They are sometimes prepared to deny anything that fails to slot neatly into their ideas of truth and justice. Above all, they are prepared to deny their own weakness or any limitation of power. They strive to satisfy their instincts. There is no greater punishment for the EIGHT than to be isolated and cut off from all possibilities of action. They like to be fully in the picture. They have a need to check up on things and are furious when outsmarted.

Their capital blindness is shamelessness. In the time-honoured list of root sins this is described as lust. It amounts to violation of another person for pleasure or for passion. Somebody is shamelessly used, taken possession of or just blotted out. Little respect is shown for another's dignity. For an EIGHT this stance can extend to most areas of life.

EIGHTs may insist on high moral standards for others without holding themselves to the same standards. They can enjoy food, alcohol or sex without feeling any guilt. They must learn to take themselves to task for the excesses which can equally dominate their worlds of work and play. They are much more likely to experience guilt when they have been unjust or untruthful.

Because of their great lust for life, EIGHTs can enjoy the exercise of power. They are always happy to stake a claim to power when it's on offer, and will expand this power base whenever possible. In a contest they are apt to confuse their inclination to get even with the search for justice. Anger makes them feel powerful.

In a bid to keep control, they can be very fussy and insistent that everything is kept in working order. In partnerships, the only people EIGHTs respect are those who put up resistance and stand their ground. They are convinced the truth comes out in a fight.

EIGHTs enjoy the pleasure of combat but they also need considerable space for themselves. They like to climb mountains and may delight in dangerous physical challenges. They bring a restless power to all their activities and in a good cause they are prepared to absorb a great deal of suffering. They will demand honesty from the people around them and will take great delight in unmasking unworthy behaviour. They must gradually learn to demand this same honesty of themselves.

EIGHTs are challenged to use their power for the establishment of justice. In particular they are invited to gather their intensity to bring about justice on behalf of those too disadvantaged to achieve it for themselves. Confession is good for the soul of the EIGHT. They need to appreciate the latent power in forgiveness. They can be remorselessly tough on themselves, blaming themselves for eventualities far beyond their jurisdiction. Forgiveness also trims their enthusiasm for humiliating others and reminds them that carrying a grudge is burdensome. They have to drop the search for revenge. They also need to make their peace with God for perceived injustices in their own life experience.

EIGHTs are challenged to give up the illusion reflected in their warrior mask. This hurls them into a contest with most of the world around them. Ultimately they have to exchange vengeance for service.

Hooks of the EIGHT

- The pleasure of vengeance for its own sake.
- Aggression and an open expression of anger.
- Excess as an antidote to boredom – far too much and far too many.

Route of integration for The Leader

See Appendix 1: The Conversion Enterprise.

EIGHTs need to encounter truth. This frees them from the blindness which prevents them from accepting their own weakness. This encounter with truth is difficult for them because they robustly resist the inner journey. They fear the child within. Their path of integration starts with an acceptance of weakness, both in themselves and in those around them. EIGHTs can then become powerfully compassionate.

The invitation to the EIGHT is to mercy – to themselves and to others. They have to learn to trust the gentle, hidden side of their nature and to curb their aggression. As they move towards unconditional acceptance they will allow for opinions and viewpoints which differ from their own. This enhances their leadership qualities.

Power is neutral. It can be a blessing or a curse. EIGHTs, if they want to move towards integration, need to monitor what they are doing to the people around them. They need to tame their own insensitivity. They often show a passion for dominance and can be blunt to the point of severe hurt. Gradually, they must stop

They despise weakness.

humiliating and intimidating the people with whom they live and work.

EIGHTs in maturity come to operate by the same standards they set for others. When they make mistakes they own them. When necessary, they should acknowledge their own possessiveness and reluctance to adapt.

There is a danger that EIGHTs over-identify with so-called masculine energy. It may be acceptable for men to be macho, but this gives women EIGHTs a particular problem. They can refuse to accept the feminine aspect of their nature or their maternal side. Male EIGHTs, for their part, need access to their own female side, instead of delegating warmth and tenderness to women.

EIGHTs have to learn to let go of their need to control and dominate other people. They are constantly checking on trivial details as part of their power play. They shun dependency. EIGHTs can therefore experience considerable difficulty in relationships.

There is a conflict between tender impulses and acquired hardness. Personal interests have to be sacrificed and EIGHTs are reluctant to do this. They have to accept their own need for space and time to be by themselves.

The fruit of the spirit for EIGHTS is innocence. This is the child within – often completely unacknowledged – which is unprotected and yet trusting. They have to learn to see this distressed child outside of themselves and look after it there, so they can also accept the defenceless child in themselves. To move towards this acceptance of weakness, the prerequisite is sincerity, which stands very close to honesty.

Redeemed EIGHTs will enjoy using their power and vitality to protect and encourage others. They have natural gifts enabling them to direct people towards their full potential. This is true leadership.

To bring about conversion and integration EIGHTs need to embrace the positive aspects of the TWO. This will help them to:

- acknowledge the tender side of their own nature – the child within. They have to own their softer, gentler feelings and share their pangs and weaknesses.
- accept that other people have their rights too. EIGHTs, as they

move towards integration, curb their tendency to bully, to ignore and to dominate others.

- learn that power is best used for people rather than against them. When appropriate they will take stands on behalf of others, encouraging them in their turn to fight their own corner.
- accept that complete self-sufficiency is an impossible goal. Inter-dependence is part of being human and power-sharing can be to the benefit of all.
- develop their instinct to be generous. Self-interest is not the highest goal and money is more than a tool of power.

The Leader: Symbols and Invitation

The symbols used are intended as a concise but accurate portrayal of the energies of the Enneagram. Here we look at appropriate symbols for the EIGHT personality.

Animal: Tiger
The tiger is a symbol of the power of the jungle. It is cunning, ferocious and cruel. They are aware of their strength, but they are prepared to wait for the right moment before using it. They are thirsty animals and the only members of the cat family to enjoy swimming. They have great resistance to pain. They are also expert at climbing trees and adapt readily to different habitats. Like the domestic cat, the tiger is naturally inquisitive and playful. It enjoys exceptional sight and hearing. The tiger is restless but essentially lazy. To kill in order to survive is its dominant motivation.

Country: Spain
Spain wears the skin of the tiger. It is the land of the bull fight – of blood and sand. It is also the territory of the benevolent dictator. People who wear this EIGHT skin love intensity and a challenge. Here the male macho image also hides feelings of inferiority and insecurity. The EIGHT is loyal to those close to them. They tend to exercise their power on behalf of others. Once the EIGHT breaks through to the realisation of the justice of God's providence, he or

she is ready to risk and live out their destiny irrespective of the consequences.

In all countries subject to oppression, or victimised by military dictatorship, where rights are ignored or suppressed, thwarted energies will ultimately seek to find expression in acts of resistance, violence or open revolution. The oppressed group will attempt to contest the might of the oppressor.

Colour: The colours of the EIGHT are black and white. Black is the absence of colour and white stands for the totality of light. There is a longing here for clarity. EIGHTs are convinced that compromise fails to deliver. They want to see life in stark contrast – friend or foe, strong or weak.

Beliefs

- I know how to fight and win.
- You have to be tough to survive.
- In the end you are on your own.
- You are either friend or foe.

Queries

- Where does the power rest?
- What do I need to do in order to get what I want?
- Will they fight me?

Childhood message: EIGHTs are likely to have drawn the conclusion early in their lives that they have entered a combative situation – even a war zone. They appraised the odds as unfair or at least highly demanding. They concluded that in this situation there was no value or reward in being weak. Authority figures may have failed to provide limits. The EIGHT personality may also have decided there was weakness around which could be exploited or at least fully tested.

Invitation: Towards mercy

EIGHTs can be ruthless to themselves and to others. They can become addicted to the delights of revenge. But in the face of injustice, they are invited to move directly to side with the weak and to redress the imbalance. For liberation they are dependent on a stark encounter with truth. This opens them to their inner journey and helps them to accept their own vulnerability. In turn this takes them on to accept the weakness of others without the need for exploitation or abuse. Then at last they can protect without needing to dominate.

Frightened by their own child within, EIGHTs will delay their inner work. They have to face up to the basic challenge of obeying the same rules they expect others to follow. They have to learn to acknowledge when they are wrong. They come to sense the wisdom and power of passive resistance.

Finding trust in God, EIGHTs move from arrogance to simplicity, from fighting to healing. Once they seek to imitate the attitude of Jesus towards injustice, they no longer need to probe and test people. They become sensitive to the needs of others. Their natural child is released.

EIGHTs warm to a love which is wholehearted, passionate and challenging. There is intensity in their commitment. They seek truth and justice for others. They confront and unmask the oppressor.

Jesus as campaigner for justice

See Appendix 2: The Nine Enlightenments.

The strength and determination of Jesus will appeal to the EIGHT personality. Jesus knew what he wanted. He expounded his mission without compromise and was always prepared to accept the consequences. The gospel story reveals him using powerful language in order to admonish his enemies. Fired up in the cause of justice and truth, he turned on the scribes and Pharisees, describing them variously as 'blind guides', 'brood of vipers' and 'white-washed sepulchres', and again, 'Woe to you, you are the blind leading the blind'.

EIGHTs in their fearlessness have this gift for confronting injustice. Jesus saw through the pretension of his enemies, parading themselves as just and holy. But he was not merely interested in delivering a public *coup d'état* in the style of a rugged EIGHT. Jesus was interested in change. He wanted to bring the Pharisees to the point of seeing the error of their ways.

Jesus knew he would pay a price for his daring. He knew he would be called to account for speaking out, even to pay the price of a brutal death. This never prevented him from taking action. He confronted the money changers who were charging the poor exorbitant rates in the temple. He was totally opposed to their cheating in a place set apart for worship. He was incensed by their hypocrisy and fearless in his anger. Jesus believed injustice should be exposed for what it is, and by his willingness to speak out against it, he became a threat to the ruling class. Confrontation in these situations was his style of communication.

Jesus' strong sense of justice and right, with his willingness to challenge the wrongdoers, is a model for the EIGHT personality. Jesus confronted his opponents in the tradition of the prophets. 'The tax-collectors and prostitutes go into the Kingdom of God before you,' he said. And he called on his followers not to compromise their consciences, even to the point of suffering and death. He urged them to stand up on the side of the weak and to take up their cause.

In the Sermon on the Mount he praised the 'Blessed ones, who hunger and thirst for justice'. But in response to violence he offered no counter-violence. He told Peter: 'All who draw the sword, will perish by the sword.' He declared strength in non-violence, allowing God to work through gentleness in the face of oppression by others. Jesus encouraged his disciples to be fearless in speaking out and willing to suffer the consequences without resorting to violence. He was personally strong, but not invulnerable. He believed in the power of powerlessness.

The gospel encounter with Jesus will help EIGHTs to guard against:

- the refusal to acknowledge pain and weakness.
- a tendency to see who has the power and move towards it.
- a reluctance to really listen and a too swift neglect of advice.
- displaying an intense and immediate anger.
- being punishing, abrasive and sarcastic.

Jesus shows EIGHTs how to rejoice in:

- their willingness to give of themselves even when they are in trouble.
- their ability to make others feel secure and happy.
- a readiness to encourage growth and independence in others.
- the deep feelings they have towards those who are suffering and poor.
- living generously in the moment.

Spur: To change from turbulent exploiters and vengeful controllers to powerful defenders of the weakest.

Way of prayer for The Leader

See Appendix 3: Prayer and the Enneagram.

The best way of prayer for the EIGHT is one of simple presence – the prayer of quiet. High-energy people and suspicious of inactivity, EIGHTs have a natural gift for living in the present and they can bring this to their prayer life – their quest to be present to God.

The EIGHT route therefore is to let go of activity and excitement, to be empty of thoughts and feelings, and to be centred in order to come into a loving presence. They are there in faith, just sitting, presenting themselves to God just as they are.

To make the inner journey, each personality type in the Enneagram system has to develop their own form of surrender. This will touch on, but move beyond, the essential gift of the type. To surrender the illusion of self, EIGHTs need to move towards freedom, away from the abuse of power and domination of others. The detachment of prayer will take them into powerlessness. Receptive and waiting, open to what may come, they will find silence their way to intimacy.

EIGHTs can bring their best powers to prayer. Pulled as they are by strong and diverse energies, they need the discipline of concentration. In set meditation, they may initially have to return to the repetition of the single thought, shortening the mantra until there is only silence.

Through their body they can allow the ordinary involvements of the day to dip away, letting themselves move deeper into the zone of the spirit. Creative movement may also work for them in the same way. In particular, they can use the sensate to contact and experience the spiritual. Through clay, for example, or some other art form such as music, they can surrender themselves and make contact with their deepest feelings and energies. They can harness the symmetry of colour and shape to close the gap between inner experience and the world outside of themselves. This route can bring them both heightened sensitivity and inner peace.

The EIGHT route to well-being

Unhealthy characteristics: aggressive, tyrannical, dictatorial, vengeful
Average characteristics: enterprising, forceful, controlling, belligerent
Redeemed characteristics: self-assertive, magnanimous, protective, courageous
Values: fair-play, justice, freedom
Time tendency: present
Strongest senses: hearing, smell
Emotion least controlled: anger
Domination: power and control
Masks: control, revenge, friendship
Problems: indecision, repression

The EIGHT surrenders

- I no longer demand that I should be able to control everything in my life.
- I let go of the belief that I need to be vengeful in order to free myself from my own pain.
- I abandon the idea that anyone who does not agree with me is against me.

The EIGHT affirmations

- I affirm that I am most fulfilled when I give my support to others.
- I say 'yes' to my tender feelings and my kind impulses.
- I now affirm that there is an authority much greater than my own.

Pilgrim path for the EIGHT personality

The Leader's route of impact

EIGHTs, as we have seen, feel comfortable on the trail to power. Seldom do they feel obliged to apologise for themselves. They have an intuitive sense of power and want to be close to the controls in order to make an impact.

EIGHTs bring energy and impetus to our world. They are the

They need to find the tender side of their nature.

instigators of change – even of revolutions. Without the spirit of the reforming EIGHT, the world would be in danger of a deadly inertia or of being trampled over by tyrants and meglomaniacs.

EIGHTs are not unduly concerned about what the rest of us think of them and they can mobilise this unusual detachment to move things along. All-or-nothing types, when you join battle with an EIGHT, the likelihood is that part of them at least is going to enjoy it. The contest enlivens them.

EIGHTs storm to good effect against injustice. For them fighting is an exciting way of engagement. Capable of standing in defiance – and in a good cause – their great gift, if they can come to it, is that they can unleash full-frontal courage on behalf of the oppressed. Their energy adds up to a total conviction.

Powerful leaders ought to enjoy empowering others. To have this impact, healthy EIGHTs have to learn to discipline their self-assertion. When they operate from this position of positive self-restraint, they can be deeply loving, protective and empowering. This is their true route of impact.

To come to this, EIGHTs need to pay attention to the gentle side of their personality. This compassionate, nurturing aspect of their character, when embraced and fuelled, enables them to bring passion to their caring. Without ego and supportive of those close to them, they can combat hard and long for those not strong enough to fight for themselves, or those threatened unjustly. EIGHTs have the potential to liberate and do great good for others.

They learn by adversity. The more they assert themselves, the more self-confident they become. But it is not enough to be passionate about who has the power. They need to be passionate in carefully selected causes and for specific people. They have the potential for physical and moral courage and for making the highest sacrifices on behalf of others. They can lead those around them to achieve goals which are valuable for everyone, for causes much larger than themselves.

God image

EIGHTs look to a powerful God who can make things happen. They are impatient with a God who hesitates, as it seems, to take up the challenge of almighty solution-provider. The powerlessness of Jesus can puzzle an EIGHT. As they come to terms with their own inner child, they may see reflections of the God who loves, is gentle and liberates.

When you meet an EIGHT

- If you promise them you will do something, try to deliver.
- Remember, EIGHTs like to know where you are coming from, so be direct.
- What feels like an outburst to you may be no more than style from an EIGHT. If you feel threatened let them know.
- Don't let them catch you lying and don't humiliate them.
- If they hurt your feelings, tell them. It may not be what they intended.
- Remember, EIGHTs look tough but they can be hurt.
- Let them know you understand what they are saying. Then there is a chance that your point of view will be listened to.

The Mediator

13

FACE NINE

The Mediator

Peacemaker, Moderator, Pacifist, Reconciler, Co-ordinator, Diplomat, Go-between, Trouble-shooter, Umpire and Comforter

Peace and love are always alive in us, but we are not always alive to peace and love.

Julian of Norwich

My way: Mediation
My statement: 'I am content.'
My centre: Gut
My passion: Laziness
My compulsion: Inactivity
My fear: Conflict
My avoidance: Conflict
My method: Peace
My need: Action
My virtue: Diligence

Gift

The gift of the NINE personality motivates them towards tolerance and mediation. They offer unconditional support and exercise a calming influence. They look for harmony and want to inspire a peaceful and comfortable life. They are accommodating and capable of true contentment. Patient and easy-going, they are talented arbitrators and are capable of putting considerable effort into their work. They are intuitive, make good listeners and can sense what is important in other people's lives.

Nothing is vitally important for the NINE. As children they may have had the experience of being overlooked – or thrust centre stage. They may have concluded that they are not important enough to be loved and they seem to belittle themselves and their own worth. They choose to be the people nobody will notice. They are often easy-going children without much self-esteem. They learn not to make too much effort and they do not show their feelings openly.

NINEs tend towards indecision and laziness. They can, however, spend a great deal of energy trying to avoid conflict. They are natural peacemakers. They want their immediate environment to be harmonious and are reluctant to counter aggravation. They postpone decisions and are willing to compromise in order to keep the peace.

NINEs are acceptant and tolerant people. They are non-judgemental and non-threatening. They can see both sides of an argument and have a natural skill for arbitration. They are unassuming and usually have a calming influence on those around them. They can also be given to daydreaming.

They find it difficult to organise their priorities and therefore they can busy themselves in non-essentials. They avoid getting excited about things. They look to the path of least resistance and keep their anger to themselves.

Being late doesn't bother the NINE personality. They enjoy being rooted to their own territory. They are honest and their agenda is usually without hidden motives. What they say is very likely to be what they mean.

They don't really trust themselves and are uneasy with compliments. They cultivate the self-image of not being very important. They opt to stay out of the limelight in case people expect too much of them. They have an inner hiding place and depend on others making the effort to approach them.

NINEs can avoid taking initiatives and are inclined to be stubborn. They may give the impression of being absent-minded, vague or bored. In distressing situations they tend to withdraw.

NINEs will be inclined to say 'yes' to most of the following statements:

- Most things in life aren't worth getting that worked up about.
- I'm a natural peacemaker and tend towards harmony in relationships.
- I like some time just to do nothing.
- I'm intuitive and sense the needs of other people.
- I generally follow the line of least resistance.
- I try to avoid conflict but I can be stubborn.
- My attitude is 'I don't let it bother me'.
- I experience some difficulty taking decisive action.
- I do what I can to preserve my energy.
- The spiritual and mystical aspects of life attract my attention.

'I am content.'

Challenges confronting The Mediator

The life task of NINEs is to unearth and develop feelings of self-worth and their own life force. They need to come to an understanding and acceptance of their real longings and agenda. Procrastination has to be challenged.

Often reluctant to reveal themselves, NINEs too easily take refuge in not knowing what it is they want. They may lack self-confidence and often prefer to adopt a background role. They opt not to draw attention to themselves and can be quite happy when inconspicuous. This leads them to neglect their precious gifts. They are prepared to merge with other people's agendas. Nevertheless, they usually respond when others invite them out of their hiding place. They sometimes harbour a deep cynicism towards life. They have to learn to challenge this mistrust.

NINEs can look for consolations in addictions. They have to guard against these. Because they can be vulnerable to the hardships and pressures of life, they can take flight in these addictions. Finding it difficult to stimulate themselves, they look to external stimuli in narcotics for consolation: food, drink, television and shopping are obvious options. In the same way they can readily use sleep as the ideal place to retreat to when life becomes arduous. They can be stubborn and adopt a style of passive aggression. Detecting these traits is central to their journey.

NINEs will often withdraw when the going gets tough. They are unlikely to think that others are interested in their problems. Fortunately, love and attention will usually help NINEs to get back on their feet again. Often NINEs will refuse to accept that they are worthy of this love – and this despite the fact that they have the gentle gift of blending, of being endlessly undemanding, loving and tender.

The capital blindness of NINE is laziness. They can be easy-going to a fault. They may have learned to numb themselves and can readily lose contact with what it is they really want. NINEs avoid conflict. When of a mind to do so, they can avoid entire realms: good and evil, duties and satisfactions, friends and relations, and most of all themselves.

They have problems in taking initiatives and mustering the

determination to see a project through. They have a tendency to be caught up and even eclipsed by secondary issues or to succumb to other people's agendas. They can be angry at being unheard or overlooked but they will still be inclined to hold back their anger rather than take a decisive stand. Resistance is their natural stance.

NINEs will seldom make the first move to establish contact. They may also avoid being tied down by others. They can find outside pressures exhausting. While outwardly composed and usually capable of having a calming effect on others, they can readily boil up inside. They spend much of their energy dealing with inner and outer conflicts. In partnerships they will switch from fusion to autonomy. Paradoxically, they can also be the most stubborn of partners.

They operate best within clearly defined guidelines or even contracts. With too much space for self-determination nothing much will happen. They can give the impression of sitting endlessly on the fence. NINEs know how to be deeply reluctant. They will sometimes adopt the attitude of just waiting in the expectancy that a solution will eventually simply materialise.

NINEs make excellent mediators and peace-keepers because their natural two-sidedness urges them to both agree and yet hold back in any given conflict situation. But, as with all the types, their personality faultline sits close to their gift. It can become their habit to express anger by pretending they didn't notice. But they are not easily provoked. An explosion will be a long time in the preparation.

Their difficulties with decision-making, anger and coming to a personal viewpoint, stem from the fact that they don't take themselves seriously enough and too often expect others to be the active agents in their lives.

NINES are challenged to confront their tendency to resignation. They have to face in specific ways their essential need to discover and develop their feelings of self-worth and inner drive. They are called on to appraise their life experience and order their priorities and commitments. To achieve this they may need for a time to become bond-slaves of the first step, taking their captivity in hand as it were, and seeking out the possibility of action at every turn, including symbolic action. As they become involved in this way and tilt at their reluctance to act and any inner sense of hopelessness, they begin to appreciate that lasting peace is delivered only through conflict. They experience at first hand that the conflict, when faced, ushers in an unexpected vitality. They also learn that the true source of authority resides within.

NINEs are challenged to defy their own reluctance and sense of insignificance, to attend to their inner voice, and to sense their own worth and unequivocal value.

Hooks of the NINE

- Holding back physical energy and anger.
- Replacing essential needs with inessential substitutes.
- Acting through habit and only at the end of the day.

They prefer not to draw attention to themselves.

Route of integration for The Mediator

See Appendix 1: The Conversion Experience.

Many NINEs are gifted but reluctant to exhibit their gifts. They have been aptly described as gentle prophets. They look towards a world where people can live in peace and harmony. This is the goal they seek for themselves and they want to extend it to all in their circle. But they try to avoid paying the price.

The fruit of conversion for the NINE is positive action. The first inclination of this personality is to hesitate and postpone decisions. They have to battle with sloth. But when they eventually reach a decision it can be packaged with a surprising clarity. They know what is required and they do it.

The positive aspects of their quest for harmony and contentment include their natural gifts for peace-making and mediation. But to move into this vital sphere with real authority they first need to experience the energising power of being wanted, of being important and of having something special to give. They have to come to know that they are loved by God in their own right. It is often a communal enterprise that will lead them to this awareness.

NINEs have to learn to encounter their innate cynicism and mistrust of life. This can take the form of an abiding lethargy that tells them that nothing really matters. They have to stop papering over the cracks. But first they need to discover their own energy source within.

The experience of an unconditional love leads them back into community so they can begin to act with purpose and precision. To move towards growth and maturity, and therefore to really enjoy themselves, NINEs have to act boldly and open themselves to risk. They have to cast off the slumber of procrastination and uncertainty. As they uncover and appreciate their own value they can start to stand up for themselves and this in turn opens them further to their own self-worth and giftedness.

It is sometimes helpful for NINEs to rage inwardly in order to unbolt and flex the inner drive they need to exercise. In this way they can get in touch with feelings which otherwise they are inclined to deny. Without hurt to others, they can free themselves to identify and engage with priorities.

NINEs like to be rooted. They have a deep longing to bring together everything that is complex and unresolved. They aspire to merge opposites and uncover new truths as they search for wholeness. This is another reason why they need to come to terms with any denial of their feelings.

NINEs should refrain from fatalism or becoming too defensive. They sometimes hide behind a passive aggression. It is a difficult but rewarding task for them to complete the projects they have begun. In this way they overcome their laziness and their conviction that nothing really matters. They free themselves as they deal with the immediate and open both to the invitation to service – which is all around them – and the realisation of the importance of their own gifts.

To bring about conversion, NINEs need to embrace the best aspects of the THREE. This will help them to:

- begin to appreciate their own value. Their prime need is to acknowledge their self-worth. NINEs cannot extend their love to others until they have learned to love and appreciate themselves.
- be responsible for their own lives. They need to move away from complacency and their tendency to drift. They have to return and face reality.
- face the negative in their lives. Avoidance should not be an end in itself. They need to acknowledge their own reluctance, and the times they are stubborn or aggressive.
- face up to conflict and tension. The line of least resistance will on some occasions need to be avoided. There is often a price to pay for peace.
- confront the tendency to escape and the habits that go with it – pills, drink, narcotics, shopping, sleep, etc. These are not the solution.

The Mediator: Symbols and Invitation

The symbols are intended as a description of the major energies of the Enneagram personality types. Here we consider appropriate symbols for type NINE.

Animal: Bear
Slow, cumbersome and peace-loving by nature, the bear remains indifferent unless provoked. However, if compelled, they can attack with speed and ferocity. For the most part, the bear believes in taking life easy. It is without natural enemies. The bear likes to take a bath every day and enjoys wandering about its immediate neighbourhood. These excursions are usually followed by long spells of rest and sleep. The person who wears this skin has a longing for everything to settle down. They are apt to experience emotions as a sign of weakness and are constantly in search of the peaceful solution. They are sometimes fascinated by psychology. For the fortunate bear, life can be viewed as one long picnic.

Country: Russia and Switzerland
The bear has become Russia's national symbol. Like the grizzly bear, Russia is powerful but tends to keep to itself. Russia has historically lagged behind most other European countries in the prosperity stakes, but we ought perhaps to be more trustful of Russia's desire for peace.

Switzerland has acquired a reputation for peacekeeping and for banking. It is another snow-packed land protected by mountains. Diligence in financial affairs mirrors the hoarding instinct of the bear. Watchmakers also thrive in Switzerland and the people who wear the bear skin are often time-conscious and natural tourists.

Colour: Gold or saffron is the NINE's colour. The gold standard is retained as a financial apex in our society. Saffron is the colour worn by Buddhist monks. Gold was presented to the child Jesus and is the colour of the highest, associated with royalty and the enlightened. Just as gold is extracted with difficulty from deep within the earth, NINEs have to mine hard for their gifts and allow them to be circulated. The golden age reflects the era of the NINE, a time of peace, contentment and harmony.

Beliefs

- Nothing is especially important.
- Others' needs are more important than mine.

Queries

- Is this the right choice?
- But just suppose that . . .?

Childhood message: NINEs may have decided at an early age that they were being neglected or disregarded, or the family 'tolerance' may have prevented expression of their anger. They found themselves occupying neutral territory between warring factions. They had the impression, perhaps, that their parents' concerns were more important than their own and nothing they could devise at that stage changed these priorities.

Invitation: Towards wholeness and love

NINEs need the experience of being important, of being wanted and having something to give. They quest for unconditional love. They want to be used and not abused. If they can experience a trust that others have in them, they can find hope and belief in themselves. This is what they long for.

To do this they have to overcome what can be regarded as cynicism, reluctance or even a passive fatalism. Their energy needs focus to prevent them from winding down and opting out. They have to recognise their own golden energy within and keep tapping into this. This is the buried energy that keeps them acting decisively. Sometimes they have to embrace risk in order to experience themselves.

NINEs seek to integrate opposites. When they are immobilised or lethargic, it is useful for them to rage about what blocks and prevents them. This can help to overcome their sadness and grief and release the obstructions.

NINEs warm to the love of friends who put them in touch with their essential goodness. When NINEs discover God's love and recognise their own real worth, this awakening uncovers a longing for wholeness. God's promixity keeps them in touch with their own essential lovableness. The Spirit can pour this love into their hearts. When convinced of their worth, they can begin to engage in the building of God's Kingdom. Response to love shows itself in action. God's love moves them on from passive reluctance to the role of activist and front runner. They become true lovers in personal and practical ways.

Jesus as patient peacekeeper

See Appendix 2: The Nine Enlightenments

Through all the intense involvements of his active life, and in his gospel of healing and forgiveness, Jesus personifies calm and peace. NINEs can identify with this characteristic of Jesus.

Even as he faced up to the most demanding moments in his life, Jesus remained peaceful. This external serenity was an expression of deep inner calm and acceptance of the will of God. It freed him for service: 'Come to me, all who labour and are heavily burdened and I will give you rest,' he promised.

But for Jesus, peace was far from indolence or a bogus harmony. Love and the Kingdom were his goals. Jesus preached a Kingdom which is at once immediate and long-term. To discover it calls for insight and patience. God's designs take time to unfold and the Kingdom's progress, like our own, comes by degrees. NINE personalities can understand this: they have the gift of patience.

NINEs can appreciate the patience of Jesus towards his disciples. The gospel story shows how they kept looking towards the instant arrival of the Kingdom which Jesus had promised. But Jesus had to constantly remind his followers that life with God takes patience. His ways are not our ways.

Sometimes the problem for the NINE is patience taken too far, causing indolence. Their failure to become involved leaves them with a poor self-image and makes them feel empty. By overcoming personal isolation, however, through engagement, mutual love and dialogue with others, they find themselves growing in new ways and moving towards an unsuspected giftedness.

NINEs need to take seriously Jesus' promise of power through the Spirit. This is the same Spirit that enthused and enlivened Jesus in his own activity. It gives people the confidence that God loves them. Each person is a special gift of God to the world. NINEs need to become aware of their own potential. They need to make a gift of their inner life to others, as Jesus constantly demonstrated.

A risk that NINEs run is of failing to discover for themselves the resources they possess. They depend too much on outside stimulation and they can fail to live in a creative way. They can allow indolence to wreak havoc in the ultimately crucial zone of their spiritual life.

With the gift of the Spirit comes an inner peace from knowing God's personal love. Then out of gratitude NINEs can move on to help others. They will know the answer to the vital question: 'Where do I serve?' In this way they progress the work of Jesus – the route of peace and reconciliation. They can then discover their capacity for leadership, their ability to link people in the cause of peace and assist others as they work through conflict and division.

NINEs have a natural gift for building community and helping others to experience its value.

The gospel encounter with Jesus will help NINEs to guard against:

- being over-involved in trivia. NINEs can lose sight of the larger picture.
- a reluctance to commit themselves and to stand firm in a difficult situation.
- a hesitancy to take responsibility for their own lives.
- a tendency to lack purpose, become lazy and procrastinate.

Jesus shows NINEs how to rejoice in:

- their role as peacemakers and their willingness to accept others.
- their capacity for fairness and an appreciation of both sides of a situation.
- an ability to be calm and to reassure others.

- a longing for unity and harmony.
- their ability to make others feel important.

Spur: To move from reluctant refuge-seeker to instigator of peaceful and harmonious ways of living.

Way of prayer for The Mediator

See Appendix 3: Prayer and the Enneagram.

Although caught at times between the attitude of peace at any price and feelings of frustration and hopelessness, NINEs can use their natural gift for peacemaking and harmonious living with a view to deepening their prayer life.

The innate style of the NINE is the prayer of simplicity. They have no need for words. In a quiet place, NINEs can just sit, be peaceful and open to God. They have no requirement for concepts, ideas or feelings.

This is the prayer of peaceful abiding, of gentle, loving attention. They can come to know the solace of being in God's presence. This is the prayer of deep surrender, of waiting and longing, of letting go and self-abandonment. The essential requirement is receptivity. God is known here in the emptiness and the darkness. This is not idleness and NINEs may often need to remind themselves that they are attending to God. A desire of the will is enough to bring them to this prayer.

Their attachment to keeping conflict suppressed can lead NINEs, as we have seen, to procrastinate and make them reluctant to set priorities. Their steadfast return to the inner centre of stillness will require discipline. The Jesus Prayer or a simple mantra can help them to achieve this focus. The discipline of communal prayer can also be beneficial.

The world of symbol and myth, or dream images, can be revealing for the NINE. Using clay or paints, for example, can help them to contact and express their feelings. Through the use of their body in prayer, they can begin to combine the power of action with the passive acceptance of contemplation.

NINEs may need to let go of their customary feelings of unworthiness. As they present themselves wholeheartedly, risking losing themselves in God, their sensitivity and serenity will increase. Through this prayer they can become aware of what they long to know – that they are deeply, unconditionally loved by God. Here they can find the grace of considered action, and instead of withdrawing, will become purposefully engaged. Recognising and prayerfully acknowledging their own gift for peacemaking, NINEs can open themselves to the discovery of areas in their lives where it is precisely this talent that is called for. These will be immediate and down-to-earth situations.

Ultimately, the test of the effectiveness of these varied methods of prayer remains the same for all personality types: Are we becoming more loving, more compassionate, more humble?

The NINE route to well-being

Unhealthy characteristics: ineffectual, obstinate, fatalistic, disorientated

Average characteristics: self-effacing, oblivious, indecisive, passive, resigned

Redeemed characteristics: contented, receptive, supportive, patient, good-natured

Values: harmony and peace

Time tendency: present

Strongest senses: hearing, smell

Emotion least controlled: anger

Domination: control

Masks: addiction/partnership, indolence

Problems: indecision

The NINE surrenders

- I no longer neglect myself and my own legitimate needs.
- I let go of my search for quick and easy solutions to my problems.
- I abandon all dependency and fear of being on my own.

They need to appreciate their own value.

The NINE affirmations

- I affirm that I am excited about my future.
- I say 'yes' to the world around me.
- I now affirm that I am a powerful and healing person.

Pilgrim path for the NINE personality

The Mediator's route of acceptance

Each of the personality routes as outlined by the Enneagram can lead to a Christlike, universal encounter through love. The way of the NINE personality in the Enneagram system is the route of gentle acceptance, of peace and non-violence.

NINEs move without threat. They can conjure up a gentle form of resistance even to the banal and the stupid. NINEs don't make enemies. They have a gift for non-violent resistance. It is their way of life. Eventually, this journey of gentle non-violence as exhibited by the NINE has to be free to lead to a universal awakening which, in Christian terms, we call the values of the Kingdom.

NINEs have to decide how they are going to make their way in this world. They sense eventually that it may not be enough just to opt for the passive. When they focus deliberately on their goal, it brings objectivity and precision which can take them into the action and further towards the reign of peace.

NINEs have the gift of being able to bring others with them. This is the secret of their style of leadership. They are personally without pretension and have a natural ability to mediate in disputes and to sort out conflicts. They are supportive healers and can bring out the best in those around them.

The redeemed NINE has allowed acceptance to bring peace and this is the essential gift they want to spread. They have discovered that even conflict is on their side. This route of reconciliation is of course a path of deepest love. Like the other routes, it calls for wholehearted conversion and courage.

God image

NINEs are happy with the God who makes few demands on them. They are content to say: 'God's in his heaven, all's well with the world.' God is an abiding presence. But this is a partial view. God is also co-protagonist. We need to co-operate with this God in the renewal of the world. Letting be has its place but it's a good deal less than the whole story. NINEs usually need to bring more energy to their relationship with God. They may need to engage God more, even to the point of contesting with God.

When you meet a NINE

- Listen to them and acknowledge them. They're often convinced they have been overlooked.
- Keep asking them questions to find out where they are coming from. Help them to focus.
- Offer them gentle encouragement as they explore their anger.
- Ask them to be specific about what they want and need.

Awareness of wing strengths may gradually become apparent.

14

INFLUENCES FROM THE WING

We must learn self-abandonment so that we can be wholly pliant in the hands of God.

Irina Tweedie

Enneagram theory points to nine specific personality types, with the suggestion that one of these types matches our own personality. But this is not to contend that each of us is restricted to one self-standing integrated type. Human nature is more flowing and diverse than that. As an attempt to explain living truth, the Enneagram is always paradoxically simple and yet complex. The wing theory of the system, which we consider briefly here, also offers scope for variation and differences.

The 'Nine Faces of God' have been presented as points on a circle. This allows for overlapping, with each energy type moving into the next. Round the circle, each type has two close neighbours or wings. The FOUR personality, for example, possesses a FIVE wing and a THREE wing. The wings are always adjacent to the main personality type. You cannot be a FOUR personality with a NINE wing, for instance.

Enneagram enthusiasts offer various wing theories. Underlying this assortment is the fact that the wings bring influences which add colour, depth and flexibility to the personality types. Our wings contribute to our unpredictability.

Some theorists suggest that the effective wing can only be one of the two types on either side of the basic personality. A SEVEN, for example, has either an EIGHT or a SIX wing, but not both. A NINE personality has either an EIGHT wing or a ONE wing, but not both. But this is hard to substantiate as a general rule.

Once you have alighted on your basic personality type, awareness of wing strengths will gradually become more apparent. Careful observation, detachment and perhaps some advice or sharing will assist. One of the wings may appear to be more applicable, a more likely fit than the other, but this may not be true in every case.

The effect of the wing adds to the variety within the personality types, not only by influencing the main type, but because the amount or proportion of wing that makes up a personality will vary significantly. For example, two people who are SEVEN types with a dominant EIGHT wing will have similar personalities. But there will also be differences and these can be attributed to the amount of EIGHT that influences the basic SEVEN personality, as well as the different contribution from the SIX wing.

The precise amount or percentage of the wing to the basic type is obviously impossible to measure. In theory, in percentage terms the impact of the wings could vary between 1 per cent and 49 per cent. Obviously a wing energy could never be more than 49 per cent without becoming the basic energy.

Another theory sometimes put forward is that in the first half of life one of the wings will be developed, and in the second half of life the other wing then exercises a dominant influence.

There is no need to be caught up in these speculations. The intention here is to encourage awareness and appreciation of wing influence on the basic personality. This process will again bring reassurance, confidence and motivation towards further progress. Awareness of the wing theory also helps in understanding the depth and variation offered by the Enneagram process.

This book has a restricted goal. As suggested at the outset, it is no more than an introduction to the Enneagram system. There is, for example, no attempt to explain here what are usually described as the sub-types or instincts. These result from a further three-way division within each of the nine basic types according to our sexual, self-preservation and social instincts. But grappling with these and other intricacies of the rich Enneagram route is best left to a more advanced treatment of the subject. The aim here is to present a synthesis and a simplification of the best of the Enneagram tradition and to put these psychological and spiritual insights in a Christian context. It is hoped that this process will help to allay any fears and basic misunderstandings about the Enneagram's validity and its use as a system to support maturity and growth.

You cannot make the journey alone.

15

ENDNOTE
A Spiritual Tool in an Age of Some Confusion

Each and every one of us is irreplaceable, like a unique masterpiece in a collection, for God is an artist who never repeats or copies himself.

Ernesto Cardenal

The path of conversion

The Enneagram of personality points us to accessible freedoms, to real truths about ourselves. The system encourages us to trust ourselves because we have particular gifts, and it spells them out. But then it abruptly reminds us not to over-estimate ourselves. We also carry around with us the shadow of our gifts. We are challenged by the interplay of the process to face up to the hidden aspects of our own personality – and their consequences. The system goes on to detail the deception in our personality. These are the energies that support our false self. Fortunately, as we have seen, it also traces the path of conversion and integration for each of the nine types.

We have classified these nine basic energies of personality as follows:

One: The Perfectionist
Two: The Giver
Three: The Achiever
Four: The Artist
Five: The Observer
Six: The Supporter

Seven: The Optimist
Eight: The Leader
Nine: The Mediator

We have also seen that one of the most valuable aspects of the system, which follows from the basic drive of each of the types, is the inner dynamic that points us to our individual path of change and conversion.

Initially, the detection process is highly individual. The benefits seem to be ours alone. At this stage we are still looking to recognise our own gifts and the blocks that curb our blessing. But we would be missing a crucial insight if we failed to keep the communal aspect of our search in perspective. The Enneagram reminds us that the path of integration is not a solitary affair.

The abandoned island

The social dynamic of the Enneagram system is highly significant. Perhaps more than any other system of personality, it rids us of the illusion that our development – psychological or spiritual – can be accomplished in isolation. If this journey of self-discovery is to be ultimately effective, it is vital to acknowledge the democratic aspect of the system. Our personal and communal systems of growth are interdependent.

The process ultimately serves as a constant reminder that we are never alone with either our gifts or our shadow. The Enneagram confirms for us – cost what it may – that no man/woman is an island. We each have a journey of self-discovery to make, but we cannot make it alone.

The paradox at the root of the Enneagram – and of our personality – has an impact not only on our psychological and emotional well-being, but also on our spiritual life. How we respond physically, mentally and emotionally can never be separated from our spiritual response. In the end, the Enneagram turns out to be primarily a tool for spiritual enrichment. It stimulates our spiritual consciousness. It frees us to love ourselves, others and God.

The journey towards spirituality

As we have seen, the Enneagram is based on the original Sufi insight that there are nine constant aspects of personality that can act either as a blessing or as a preventative to individuals as they open up their search for truth, self and God. This map of guidance was described by the Sufis as the 'Face of God'. Each of the nine personality fields was viewed as a mirror image, lights reflected back from the one Divine source.

In the Christian tradition, the Jesuits in particular – although by no means exclusively – have been at pains to demonstrate that this nine-sided wisdom of the Enneagram can be adapted to the traditional Christian route of spiritual guidance. In a practical way the system can help us to come to terms with the two-sidedness of our personality: the blessed and the broken within each of us.

The Enneagram has been presented here as a spiritual tool, as a way of seeing into and beyond ourselves, a way of looking at reality and at God without being caught up in a hypnotic, mirror image of ourselves. Physical and mental well-being and robust spirituality turn out to be earthed in reality.

The spiritual life of most people needs the backing of self-knowledge. On a journey of true religion, ideally, we discover who we are. We come full face to God. We should eventually ask: 'So who am I in God?' And ideally we would come to know the answer. And as we acquire this knowledge we discover to our great relief that there is less and less need for us to overstate ourselves. This is a real stage on the path of conversion.

The Enneagram can have this impact. It offers us a glimpse of the meaning of self. In doing so, it cuts us to size – nothing more, nothing less. We have seen how each of us at best is no more than a sliver of the whole, a glint (and that no more than one ninth) of the total aspect.

The system turns out to be a constant reminder not to take ourselves too seriously. We are all in urgent need of humour, of self-abandonment and of endless conversion. The paths we are on – the personalities we inhabit – limited and yet real, are no more than windows to a much larger world.

The Enneagram teaches us to trust our roots, to relax and

abandon the illusory. We come from divine origins. St Paul wanted us to ponder who we are: 'Hidden with Christ in God.' Our richness, ultimately, is not found in ourselves but in our godly roots. These Kingdom values dawn slowly. Our individual Enneagram style turns out to be a window of darkness. From it we perceive a world of scarcity. But the world given by God, the Kingdom vision, is a realm of abundance. We are invited to join the banquet.

The Enneagram is an integration system. If it is true, it comes from the Holy Spirit, the source of all being. In so far as it is true, it will have the potential to open us up to a greater compassion, directed towards both ourselves and those who journey with us.

Spirituality goes deeper than self-help. Self-help shows us how to work on our well-worn rut. Spirituality points us to our rut, shows us how to work on it, and then encourages us to hand it over. Self-help is about self-control. Spirituality takes over when control is eventually abandoned. It is God ultimately who takes us along this path and it calls for grace. We don't change ourselves, we are changed.

In the end, the individual spiritual life is about who we truly are, who we truly become. The Enneagram assists us directly in this search. It is a spiritual tool in an age in urgent need of enlightenment. True religion points to the order that gives life value. And the Enneagram, like all spiritual routes, directs us back to the mystery called love and invites us to stay on this path.

Finally, if this book has encouraged some readers on their journey of discovery, much has been achieved. It only remains for me to thank you for your patience and to encourage you further in your life-long search.

God helps those who help themselves.

APPENDIX 1
The Conversion Enterprise

Believe that life is worth living and your belief will help create the fact.

William James

After looking at the basic descriptions of the nine Enneagram types, we need to reflect on the central dilemma facing each type. It is also important to consider how each type comes to terms with change and conversion.

We are all called to wholeness and integration. Carl Jung called this process 'individuation.' Christians sense they are also called to holiness. But, of course, it's not necessary to be familiar with the Enneagram system of personality for us to begin the journey towards maturity or to become an enlightened Christian. Day-to-day living, however, reveals that the Enneagram system attempts to express what spiritually mature people have always intuitively come to understand and to live out. Our ultimate maturity and redemption is God's grace – the fruit of our surrender, the consequence of our collapse back into God who is our centre.

But it is also a fact of life that our individual growth has to be worked for. The Enneagram is continually reminding us – and this is particularly true for the early part of our journey – that God helps those who help themselves. We have work to do, choices to make, habits to form, and as we progress along this path we open ourselves to the possibility of further growth and grace.

The Enneagram system can help us to detect the particular zone where our individual conversion enterprise needs to take place. Irrespective of our personality, most of us, as we set out on this journey towards growth and holiness, are initially inexperienced, immature and in need.

No personality type, no particular Enneagram number, is better off, or worse off, than any other type. There is a personality equality at play here. The system is attractively democratic. Everyone has their investment – no more, no less. Each of us is restricted and deficient, and at the same time we pulsate in our different potentials.

The nine-faced system of the Enneagram highlights not only the zone where we are most in need of growth and redemption, but how in reality we can begin to apply this conversion process. The system offers us a signpost to the path along which we need to journey. Each of us faces a personal invitation to growth, stemming from our individuality. We are urged to confront our personal pitfall or compulsion, and, as we do so, we progress along the path of change and conversion.

All of us have a major virtue and a dominant shadow side to our personality. These aspects are interdependent and they give us energy. On the shadow side, all of us have our limitations. The system teaches us that most of these can be traced to one big obsession. The earlier we recognise this obsession, the sooner we have something tangible to work with.

Redemption or conversion in this sense is also about seeing through our own game. We all operate from mixed motives. We do most things in our life not for others but for ourselves. When it comes to the crunch we are usually short on real compassion – that style of giving which is emphatically without self. But the Enneagram offers us an insight which can help us to build on firmer ground. It invites us to call our illusions by name. If we can uncover at least our major mask, and some of the games we play which pivot around our basic deception, then part of our masquerade can fall and may give way to genuine compassion.

The Enneagram underwrites the spiritual journey, and in doing so reveals to us the dark side of our gift. There is a tap root that obstructs our path. It is constant and yet difficult to identify and acknowledge.

Here are the nine root blocks or compulsions (sins, in the classic sense) according to the nine types:

One: Perfectionist – Anger
Two: Giver – Pride
Three: Achiever – Deceit
Four: Artist – Envy
Five: Observer – Avarice
Six: Supporter – Fear
Seven: Optimist – Gluttony
Eight: Leader – Lust
Nine: Peacemaker – Laziness

For each Enneagram type there is a conversion strategy that needs to be embraced if we are to come to terms with our basic compulsion. When we choose this option, we begin to deal directly with the core sin that blocks our particular personality type.

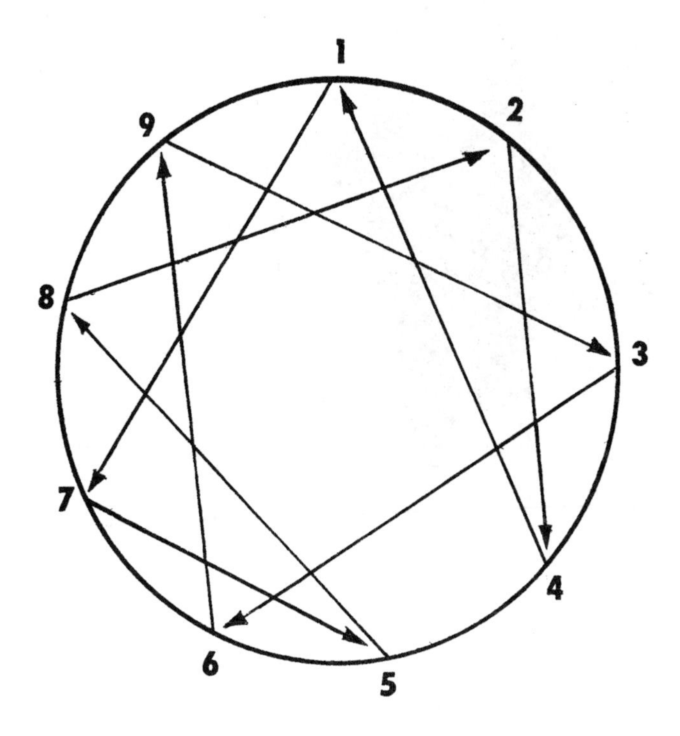

To be of value, the system must influence
our day-to-day journey.

APPENDIX 2
The Nine Enlightenments

Man is more interesting than men. God made him and not them in his image. Each one is more precious than all.
André Gide

The energies at play in the Enneagram system can be viewed as nine aspects of God.

Christians see Jesus as a portrait of God. He is God become man, the human face of God, the revelation in human form of the Trinity, the expression of divine love. As the image of the invisible God, Christ not only represents God, but is also the essence of the world. In this sense the Enneagram can be viewed as an icon of the face of Christ, who in turn is the 'face of God' as well as the 'face of the true man'. In that Jesus realised true humanity and therefore true personhood, he moved beyond the limitation of one personality type.

As we have seen, according to the Enneagram, each personality has its own compulsion – an erroneous way of living. The compulsion is a positive quality – but exaggerated. A journey of limitation is turned into an ultimate route. This is done at the cost of failing to be an integrated person.

The gospel demonstrates that Christ experienced all nine temptations of the Enneagram and responded with all nine enlightenments or liberations of the system. In the gospel record we see the Christ without compulsion, without sin.

In our egocentric culture it is easy to project God as an image of ourself. The Enneagram helps us to cut through this illusion. It opens us up to our own limited bias, our compulsive way of looking at life.

Jesus is the image of the person who is challenged to integration and wholeness by God, and who succeeds. Jesus reaches the human summit. All of us, therefore, in our individal type, can orientate ourselves to Christ. Jesus accepted all nine forms of human personality and lived them through without their compulsive edge. Christ is thus the model of integration.

Each of the nine types in the Enneagram system can be related directly to some aspect of Jesus. To do this we can draw on the evidence of the gospel narrative and gospel values. We will see how the nine Enneagram personality types are present in Jesus. We can detect the trap which lurks behind each gift and we will see how Jesus, in his living response, avoided the block, freeing himself from the compulsion. This gospel encounter should serve not only as a reminder of the Enneagram types, including the positive and negative aspects of personality, but also as an insight into the self of Jesus.

It may be useful to recall at this point that unless the Enneagram system is operative in ordinary living, unless it exerts a challenge in our daily circumstance, influencing our day-to-day journey, then it remains of limited value. It is intended to be experiential, living, energising and for real. Only when we see and feel the system in action can we know it and harness it to our own efforts to grow.

We put on a mask to present ourselves to the world.

APPENDIX 3
Prayer and the Enneagram

Prayer does not blind us to the world, but it transforms our vision of the world, and makes us see it, all people, and all of humankind, in the light of God.

Thomas Merton

The Enneagram brings us individually to an awareness of our giftedness and of our compulsion. This insight into who we are – and who we are not – helps us to sit lightly both to our treasure and to our weakness. The Enneagram demonstrates how each of us develops a preoccupation with a certain style of energy. We put on a mask in order to present ourselves to the world, and at the same time to defend ourselves.

In prayer we attempt to come before God as we really are. This is God's invitation – to come without our mask. There is no prayer unless we allow God to be active in our lives. The requirement is receptivity, stillness before God, abandonment.

All the great religions suggest there are three basic directions of prayer:

- from the outside in
- from the inside out
- in the void

In the first type, something from the outside reaches us – perhaps a text from scripture, a hymn, a litany, a picture, an icon or a symbol.

In the second type of prayer we sit quietly and let whatever is already there within come into our consciousness. We can allow our inner moods and feelings to develop and then attempt to express them through words or through art forms such as painting or dance.

In the third type, we make use of the emptiness. All images – from inside or outside – are allowed to sink away as we relax into a stillness which is without object.

These three routes or dynamics of prayer can be related directly to the three energy centres of the Enneagram. The route which comes most naturally to us can be determined by the centre that has primary control for each individual. This means that head people (FIVE, SIX and SEVEN types) are naturally inclined to seek information from the outside. Heart people (TWO, THREE and FOUR types) will automatically seek information from the inside, while the intuitive (EIGHT, NINE and ONE types) or gut people, will find their favoured route is towards emptiness, the void.

Teachers of prayer methods rightly point out that this system is preparatory. It is an accurate preliminary route that will help us initially on our inner journey. But they warn that if it is followed too closely, in the long run it could become a pitfall. The reason for this may be obvious. We are dealing here with prayer, which is always in the end an endowment to the one who prays. It is the Spirit who teaches us to pray. Prayer, therefore, is always ultimately a gift. The pray-er is eventually caught up by the Spirit. This is God's grace in action.

In this sense, all personality types, as they are coaxed along the inner journey, are likely to be stretched beyond their natural stance. This movement may be essential for them if further growth is to take place. Prayer – like life – eventually invites us to go where we have not been before. But this is not to deny the initial benefit of accepting and developing our natural inclination according to temperament and personality as we discover it through the Enneagram system.

At the beginning of the inner journey, it is valid to ask who we are, and how best, in a natural way, each of us can be with our God. The answer will help us to take the first steps on the journey which is the real meaning of our life.

Bibliography and Suggested Reading

Beesing, Maria OP, Nogosek, Robert J. CSC and O'Leary, Patrick H. SJ, *The Enneagram: A Journey of Self Discovery*, Dimension Books, 1984.

Bergin, Eilis and Fitzgerald, Eddie, *The Enneagram*, SBD Media, 1992.

Hannan, Peter SJ, *Nine Faces of God*, The Columba Press, 1992.

Kelley, St Mary Helen OSC, Skin Deep, Designer Clothes by God, Monastery of St Clare, Memphis, Tennessee, 1990.

Linden, Anne and Spalding, Murray, *The Enneagram and NLP*, Metamorphous Press, 1994.

McNulty, Sr Elizabeth Welsh, *Planted in Love*, St Paul's, 1995.

Metz, Barbara SND and Burchill, John OP, *The Enneagram and Prayer*, Dimension Books, 1987.

Nogosek, Robert J. CSC, *Nine Portraits of Jesus*, Dimension Books, 1987.

Riso, Don Richard, *The Enneagram: Discovering Your Personality Type*, Thorsons, HarperCollins, 1987.

Rohr, Richard and Ebert, Andreas, *Discovering the Enneagram*, Crossroad Publishing, 1990.

Rohr, Richard, *Enneagram II*, Gracewing, Fowler Wright Books, 1995.

Thomson, Clarence, *Parables and the Enneagram*, Crossroad Publishing, 1996.

Tickerhoff, Revd Bernard, *Conversion and the Enneagram*, Dimension Books, 1991.

Webb, Karen, *Principles of the Enneagram*, Thorsons, HarperCollins, 1996.

Zuercher, Suzanne OSB, *Enneagram Spirituality*, Ave Maria Press, 1993.

The Tumble Trust

David Mahon, founder of the community group, Tumble Trust, holds regular workshops on the Enneagram. He would like to thank members of the Tumble Trust who have participated in these workshops over many years. Details about future workshops are available from: Tumble Trust, 7 Grammar School Road, Warrington, Cheshire, WA4 1JN (Tel: 01925–635662).
E.mail: davidmahon@tumbletrust.freeserve.co.UK
Website: www.tumbletrust.com